Table of Contents

Steps for Learning Spelling Words

1. Look carefully at the spelling word.
2. Say the spelling word out loud.
   - How many syllables do you hear?
   - What consonant sounds do you hear?
   - What vowel sounds do you hear?
3. Check the word for spelling patterns.
4. Spell the word out loud.
5. Cover the spelling word.
6. Write the spelling word from memory.
7. Check the spelling word.
8. Repeat as needed.

Spelling Week 1 – Words with a Short *a* Sound

Say each word out loud. Listen for the short ***a*** sound.

Copy and spell each word three times using colours of your choice.

1. gravity ____________ ____________ ____________
2. attach ____________ ____________ ____________
3. glance ____________ ____________ ____________
4. canvas ____________ ____________ ____________
5. adventure ____________ ____________ ____________
6. clasp ____________ ____________ ____________
7. rapid ____________ ____________ ____________
8. athlete ____________ ____________ ____________
9. actor ____________ ____________ ____________
10. fact ____________ ____________ ____________

Brain Stretch

- Create a word search puzzle based on the spelling words.
- On a piece of paper, write a sentence using each spelling word.

Spelling Week 1 – Words with a Short *a* Sound

actor	**adventure**	**athlete**	**attach**	**canvas**
clasp	**fact**	**glance**	**gravity**	**rapid**

1. Fill in the blank using the best spelling word from the list.

   a) On the moon, astronauts float because there is very little ____________________.

   b) It is a ____________________ that rain is needed for most plants to grow.

   c) When it was my turn to go onstage, I had a ____________________ heartbeat.

   d) My cousin Jenny is a fast runner. She's a very good ____________________.

   e) The spider was able to ____________________ its web to the railing and the tree.

   f) I perform plays because I want to be an ____________________ when I grow up.

   g) My grandma uses a sparkly ____________________ to hold her sweater on.

   h) When I'm waiting for lunchtime, I often ____________________ at the clock.

   i) Sandy is painting a beach scene with acrylic paints on a ____________________.

   j) The brave children went on an ____________________ to the old haunted cabin.

Brain Stretch

How many spelling words can you fit into one sentence and still make sense? Give it a try!

Spelling Week 1 – Word Study

1. Circle the word with a short ***a*** sound.

a) scrap   scrape   b) tape   tap

c) lake   lack   d) sham   shame

e) What did you notice about the words that do not have a short ***a*** sound?

____

2. Unscramble the spelling word. Write the word on the line.

a) chatat ____________   b) caft ____________   c) pirad ____________

d) tgavryi ____________   e) vnaacs ____________   f) hatteel ____________

g) ctrao ____________   h) lenagc ____________   i) lspac ____________

3. Draw a line from the spelling word to its correct meaning.

a) glance	very quick or fast
b) attach	an interlocking device used to fasten things together
c) adventure	something that is known to be true
d) rapid	to join things together
e) fact	an unusual and exciting activity or experience
f) clasp	to take a brief look

Spelling Week 1 – Word Study

1. Use the word list below to look for the words in the puzzle.

   Circle the word in the word search puzzle. Then cross out the word in the list.

R	A	B	B	I	T	C	O	J
G	C	A	M	C	O	V	A	L
B	A	N	A	N	A	V	H	A
A	N	T	T	C	H	J	A	S
S	V	R	C	U	S	C	P	T
A	A	J	H	Q	X	E	P	T
T	S	D	A	N	C	E	Y	P
I	Y	I	L	F	A	X	P	A
N	S	D	A	C	T	O	R	C
A	F	L	A	S	H	U	Z	K

actor	**banana**	**canvas**	**dance**	**flash**	**happy**
last	**match**	**oval**	**pack**	**rabbit**	**satin**

2. Underline the words that have a short ***a*** sound.

   a) paint slap take aim laugh flappy

   b) careful blanket taller stairs unfair sandwich

   c) wrapper staple frame package taffy crabby

Spelling Week 2 – Words with a Short *e* Sound

Say each word out loud. Listen for the short ***e*** sound.

Copy and spell each word three times using colours of your choice.

1. address ________ ________ ________
2. ancestor ________ ________ ________
3. distress ________ ________ ________
4. heroic ________ ________ ________
5. entrance ________ ________ ________
6. peculiar ________ ________ ________
7. arrest ________ ________ ________
8. kept ________ ________ ________
9. venture ________ ________ ________
10. permit ________ ________ ________

Spelling Tip

The short ***e*** sound can be spelled with ***ai*** (*said*) or ***ie*** (*friend*).

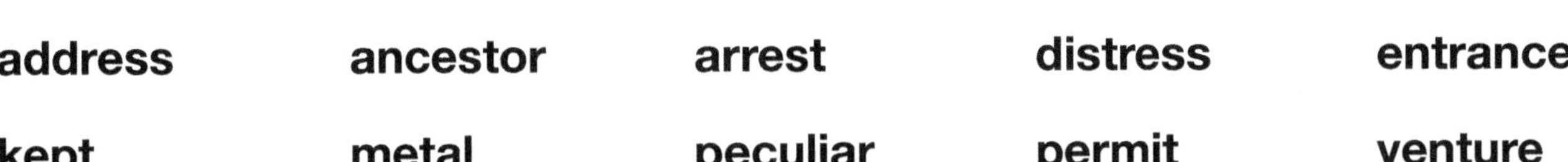

Spelling Week 2 – Words with a Short *e* Sound

address	**ancestor**	**arrest**	**distress**	**entrance**
kept	**metal**	**peculiar**	**permit**	**venture**

1. Fill in the blank using the best spelling word from the list.

   a) The big bell is made from ____________________ so it will ring for a long time.

   b) I write my return ____________________ on the envelope before I mail it out.

   c) The newest flavour of potato chips have a ____________________ smell.

   d) Tammy waited for me by the ____________________ to the park.

   e) Carter would not ____________________ himself to drop out of the race early.

   f) We found out an ____________________ of ours was a butler for the queen.

   g) The people hope the police will catch the thief and ____________________ him.

   h) Whenever grandma found four leaf clovers, she ____________________ in a book.

   i) The poor dog was stuck in the mud and was in great ____________________.

   j) At five weeks old, the fox kits were able to ____________________ out of their den.

Brain Stretch

How many spelling words can you fit into one sentence and still make sense? Give it a try!

Spelling Week 2 – Word Study

1. Underline the words that have a short ***e*** sound.

a)	kettle	sheet	spell	ate	letters	felt
b)	eight	leopard	teller	monkey	feather	shell
c)	drove	breakfast	weak	lemon	reuse	health
d)	barrel	layers	mean	tent	elephant	cheat
e)	dent	berry	sheep	slept	weight	rest

2. Circle the word with the short ***e*** sound that makes the most sense.

   Write the word in the sentence.

   a) Erin ______________ to the library to get books about horses. (went sent)

   b) Todd's ________________ snake has beautiful green eyes. (best pet)

   c) When she is tired, our dog stretches out on the comfy _______________. (deck carpet)

   d) My new skateboard is my favourite birthday _______________. (present pheasant)

3. The word ***left*** can have two meanings.

   Write a sentence to show each meaning of the word ***left***.

   ____

   ____

Spelling Week 2 – Word Study

address	**ancestor**	**arrest**	**distress**	**entrance**
kept	**metal**	**peculiar**	**permit**	**venture**

1. Write the correct spelling word from the list to match the clue.

a) A solid material that is usually shiny and can be melted and shaped in molds ____________________

b) The way into a place ____________________

c) Strange, odd, or unusual ____________________

d) A risky or daring journey or task ____________________

e) A relative that lived long ago ____________________

f) The specific details of where someone lives ____________________

g) To take someone into custody ____________________

h) To allow something to be done or to occur ____________________

i) Had or retained possession of something ____________________

j) What you do with cards you can't use in a card game ____________________

2. Write a word that rhymes with the given word. The rhyming words do not have to be spelled in the same way.

a) less ______________ b) swell ______________ c) felt______________

d) trench ______________ e) mend ______________ f) letter ______________

Spelling Week 3 – Words with a Short *i* Sound

Say each word out loud. Listen for the short ***i*** sound.

Copy and spell each word three times using colours of your choice.

1. bandit ____________ ____________ ____________
2. deposit ____________ ____________ ____________
3. centimetre ____________ ____________ ____________
4. dimple ____________ ____________ ____________
5. alligator ____________ ____________ ____________
6. mixture ____________ ____________ ____________
7. garlic ____________ ____________ ____________
8. apricot ____________ ____________ ____________
9. chicken ____________ ____________ ____________
10. English ____________ ____________ ____________

Brain Stretch

- Create a word search puzzle based on the spelling words.
- On a piece of paper, write a sentence using each spelling word.

Spelling Week 3 – Words with a Short *i* Sound

alligator	**apricot**	**bandit**	**centimetre**	**chicken**
deposit	**dimple**	**English**	**garlic**	**mixture**

1. Fill in the blank using the best spelling word from the list.

a) I love the look of an ____________________. It is small, round, orange, and fuzzy.

b) Ted was a nice cowboy for Halloween, and I was a mean ____________________.

c) To make perfect pancake batter, you need a slightly lumpy ____________________.

d) My dad made crunchy ____________________ bread to go with our pasta dinner.

e) I volunteered to help a refugee girl in my class learn ____________________.

f) When my baby sister smiles, her cute ____________________ shows in her cheek.

g) One ____________________ is equal to three-quarters of an inch.

h) Tomorrow, I will go to the bank to ____________________ my birthday money.

i) Ben has a pet ____________________ named Alice, and she lays one egg each day.

j) Carly was afraid of the ____________________ in the big pond at the zoo.

Brain Stretch

How many spelling words can you fit into one sentence and still make sense?
Give it a try!

Spelling Week 3 – Word Study

1. Circle the word with the short ***i*** sound that makes the most sense.

   Write the word in the sentence.

   a) Manny likes to ________________ while he draws and paints. (knit   whistle)

   b) Pam saw the same throne that ________________ Henry of England sat on. (King   Big)

   c) A grape accidentally got ________________ under my shoe. (swished   squished)

2. Homophones are words that sound the same but are spelled differently.

   Write the homophone for the given word.

   a) it's __________   b) nit __________   c) witch __________

   d) billed __________   e) in __________   f) links __________

3. How many syllables does the word have? Write the number beside the word.

   a) friendship __________   b) hippopotamus __________   c) ditch __________

4. The word ***fit*** can have two meanings.

   Write a sentence to show each meaning of the word ***fit***.

   ____

   ____

Across

3. bird that lays eggs that humans eat

5. large reptile that often pretends it's a log

7. small skin depression, usually in cheeks

8. put money into a safe bank account

10. substance made by mixing substances

Down

1. an Old West word for robber or thief

2. 1 metre contains 100 of these

4. small bulb used to flavour savoury foods

6. small fuzzy orange fruit

9. language used in many countries of the world

Spelling Week 4 – Words with a Short *o* Sound

Say each word out loud. Listen for the short ***o*** sound.

Copy and spell each word three times using colours of your choice.

1. rhombus __________ __________ __________
2. lodge __________ __________ __________
3. copper __________ __________ __________
4. across __________ __________ __________
5. dolphin __________ __________ __________
6. monster __________ __________ __________
7. oxen __________ __________ __________
8. fossil __________ __________ __________
9. solve __________ __________ __________
10. bother __________ __________ __________

Brain Stretch

- Create a word search puzzle based on the spelling words.
- On a piece of paper, write a sentence using each spelling word.

Spelling Week 4 – Words with a Short *o* Sound

across	**bother**	**copper**	**dolphin**	**fossil**
lodge	**monster**	**oxen**	**rhombus**	**solve**

1. Fill in the blank using the best spelling word from the list.

    a) In pioneer times, teams of ____________________ pulled ploughs and wagons.

    b) The old pennies were made of shiny ____________________.

    c) My favourite animal is the ____________________ because they are smart and playful.

    d) A diamond shape has four equal sides and is also called a ____________________.

    e) My dad is working. Let's play outside so we don't ____________________ him.

    f) At the beach today, I found a really nice shell ____________________.

    g) A beaver built a huge ____________________ in the pond at my uncle's place.

    h) Tom walked ____________________ the log to get to the other side of the creek.

    i) Mom made a stuffed ____________________ toy for my baby brother.

    j) Shhhhhh! The detective is about to ____________________ the mystery!

Brain Stretch

How many spelling words can you fit into one sentence and still make sense?
Give it a try!

Spelling Week 4 – Word Study

1. Circle the word with the short ***o*** sound that makes the most sense.

   Write the word in the sentence.

   a) Sara likes to cook in a big ____________ pot. (copper   monster)

   b) Farmers often used ______________ to pull boats along the river bank. (dolphins   oxen)

   c) My sister thinks there is a ____________ in her closet at night. (monster   fossil)

   d) I need help to _____________ this math problem. (bother   solve)

2. Write a word that rhymes with the given word. The rhyming word does not have to be spelled in the same way.

a) thought ______________	b) clock ______________	c) bother ______________
d) rocks ______________	e) drop ______________	f) cough ______________
g) caught ______________	h) loss ______________	i) box ______________

3. Circle the words that have a short ***o*** sound.

a)	school	bossy	lower	tonic	goal	softly
b)	tropical	brown	crow	glob	blond	store
c)	snooze	pocket	long	ghost	narrow	hospital

Spelling Week 2 – Word Study

across	**bother**	**copper**	**dolphin**	**fossil**
lodge	**monster**	**oxen**	**rhombus**	**solve**

1. Write the correct spelling word from the list to match the clue.

a) A very large working animal similar to a bull ____________________

b) To find an answer to, or explanation for, or way of effectively dealing with a problem or mystery ____________________

c) An orange-coloured precious metal ____________________

d) A beaver house, or a meeting place for a club ____________________

e) An imaginary creature that frightens children ____________________

f) A geometric figure shaped like a diamond ____________________

g) A rock impression of a long-dead plant or animal ____________________

h) To worry, disturb, or upset a person or animal ____________________

i) From one side of something to the other ____________________

j) An extremely intelligent aquatic mammal ____________________

2. Unscramble the spelling word. Write the correct spelling on the line.

a) hidlopn ____________ b) srcaos ____________ c) peprco____________

d) silofs ____________ e) trobeh ____________ f) mbhrsou ____________

Spelling Week 5 – Words with a Short *u* Sound

Say each word out loud. Look at the different letters that make the short ***u*** sound.

Copy and spell each word three times using colours of your choice.

1. muffin ______ ______ ______
2. crumble ______ ______ ______
3. knuckle ______ ______ ______
4. subject ______ ______ ______
5. nugget ______ ______ ______
6. husband ______ ______ ______
7. umbrella ______ ______ ______
8. jungle ______ ______ ______
9. pumpkin ______ ______ ______
10. vulture ______ ______ ______

Spelling Tip

Words with ***o*** can have a short ***u*** sound (*Monday, month, mother*).

Spelling Week 5 – Words with a Short *u* Sound

crumble	**husband**	**jungle**	**knuckle**	**muffin**
nugget	**pumpkin**	**subject**	**umbrella**	**vulture**

1. Fill in the blank using the best spelling word from the list.

   a) My grandfather found a tiny gold ____________________ in the creek.

   b) Science is my favourite ____________________ at school this year.

   c) We always carve a huge ____________________ for Halloween.

   d) We make a dessert out of bananas and we ____________________ cookies on top.

   e) Dad scraped his ____________________ on the brick wall outside and it bled.

   f) Panthers, monkeys, and many other animals live in the ____________________.

   g) Sam ate a chocolate chip banana ____________________ for a snack.

   h) Mrs. Wong's ____________________ gave us vegetables from his garden.

   i) Cam forgot his ____________________ on the bus so he got very wet.

   j) A ____________________ eats only scraps of dead animals that other animals left.

Brain Stretch

How many spelling words can you fit into one sentence and still make sense?
Give it a try!

Spelling Week 5 – Word Study

1. Circle the words that do **not** have a short ***u*** sound.

a) punch	aloud	touch	rough	though
b) scuttle	butter	pounce	rude	cough
c) stuff	spout	cute	sponge	lunge
d) crouch	thump	crumble	through	guess

2. Put the given letter or letters with the part word and say the word out loud. Circle any letters that make complete words. Write all the complete words on the line. Cross out the letters that don't make complete words.

Examples: **d m tr ouble** — **d**ouble **m**ouble **tr**ouble

b f t ox — **b**ox **f**ox **t**ox

a) **b fl v** utter

____

b) **gl k m** ove

____

c) **c gr d** ouch

____

d) **bl p th** under

____

e) **br fl p** op

____

f) **c m th** ough

____

Spelling Week 5 – Word Study

1. Use the word list below to look for the words in the puzzle.

   Circle the word in the word search puzzle. Then cross out the word in the list.

C	U	D	D	L	E	A	X	S
O	E	I	D	L	M	N	O	N
B	R	P	E	C	C	O	Z	U
U	F	J	C	R	U	M	B	G
T	U	R	O	U	P	S	O	A
T	Z	T	U	F	T	E	R	G
O	Z	U	N	D	E	R	H	E
N	Y	M	U	F	F	I	N	H
P	U	P	P	Y	K	M	B	J
D	R	T	T	L	T	U	G	Z

button	**crumb**	**cuddle**	**cup**	**fuzzy**	**muffin**
nut	**puppy**	**snug**	**tuft**	**tug**	**under**

2. Write a word that rhymes with the word below. The word does not have to be spelled the same to rhyme.

   a) bunch ______________ b) rough ______________ c) tummy ______________

   d) crumble ______________ e) blunder ______________ f) lumpy ______________

Spelling Week 6 – Words with a Long *a* Sound

Say each word out loud. Listen for the long ***a*** sound.

Copy and spell each word three times using colours of your choice.

1. decade ____________ ____________ ____________
2. frame ____________ ____________ ____________
3. able ____________ ____________ ____________
4. display ____________ ____________ ____________
5. nail ____________ ____________ ____________
6. elevator ____________ ____________ ____________
7. chain ____________ ____________ ____________
8. generate ____________ ____________ ____________
9. became ____________ ____________ ____________
10. scale ____________ ____________ ____________

Spelling Tips: The long ***a*** sound can be spelled with

- letters ***ai*** (*trail*)
- letter ***a*** with a consonant and ***e*** (*earthquake*)
- letters ***ay*** (*delay*)

Spelling Week 6 – Words with a Long *a* Sound

able	**became**	**chain**	**decade**	**display**
elevator	**frame**	**generate**	**nail**	**scale**

1. Fill in the blank using the best spelling word from the list.

   a) I learned in school that a ____________________ is ten years.

   b) The scientist waited for the machine to ____________________ the new robot.

   c) In class, we will ____________________ all our projects for our parents to see.

   d) Our puppy tried very hard, but was not ____________________ to climb the steps.

   e) Max likes to ride the ____________________ in our apartment building.

   f) I slipped a photo of my cat Percy into my new picture ____________________.

   g) Around her neck, Cindy wears a silver ____________________ with a heart on it.

   h) I broke my ____________________ when I tried to rip open that box.

   i) The caterpillar that we found last week ____________________ a pretty moth.

   j) The vet weighed my pet rat on a small ____________________.

Brain Stretch

How many spelling words can you fit into one sentence and still make sense? Give it a try!

Spelling Week 6 – Word Study

1. Say the word out loud. Underline the words with the long ***a*** sound.

a)	stair	meal	take	whale	beach
b)	shape	fall	lazy	soak	crate
c)	taste	seat	grain	real	many
d)	grade	lark	make	cheat	away
e)	space	collar	hair	drama	aim

2. Write the letters of the alphabet that have a long ***a*** sound in their name.

____

3. Write the numbers between 1 and 100 that have a long ***a*** sound in their name.

____

____

____

____

Spelling Week 6 – Word Study

1. Use the word list below to look for the words in the puzzle.

   Circle the word in the word search puzzle. Then cross out the word in the list.

S	T	E	A	K	B	C	X	N
Z	R	I	D	A	L	E	O	A
Y	A	W	A	V	E	O	P	V
B	C	X	C	A	I	I	R	A
E	H	W	I	T	S	S	A	L
A	E	T	R	A	I	N	Y	G
R	Q	Y	M	K	G	D	F	E
C	R	A	T	E	X	L	I	H
I	E	M	A	I	L	M	B	J
D	R	X	R	A	Y	U	G	Z

ache	**bear**	**crate**	**dale**	**email**	**naval**
pray	**steak**	**take**	**train**	**wave**	**xray**

2. Write a word that rhymes with the word below. The word does not have to be spelled the same to rhyme.

   a) fair ______________ b) lake ______________ c) aim ______________

   d) paste ______________ e) bay ______________ f) stain ______________

Spelling Week 7 – Words with a Long *e* Sound

Say each word out loud. Look at the different letters that make the long **e** sound.

Copy and spell each word three times using colours of your choice.

1. kilometre __________ __________ __________
2. really __________ __________ __________
3. relief __________ __________ __________
4. become __________ __________ __________
5. complete __________ __________ __________
6. secret __________ __________ __________
7. delete __________ __________ __________
8. breeze __________ __________ __________
9. fifteen __________ __________ __________
10. release __________ __________ __________

Spelling Tips: The long **e** sound can be spelled with

- letter ***e*** by itself, and ***e*** followed by a ***consonant* + *e*** (*evil, event*)
- letters ***ee***, ***ea***, and ***ie*** (*steel, beach, shield*)
- letters ***y*** and ***ey*** (*puppy, donkey*)

Spelling Week 7 – Words with a Long *e* Sound

become	**breeze**	**complete**	**delete**	**fifteen**
kilometre	**really**	**release**	**relief**	**secret**

1. Fill in the blank using the best spelling word from the list.

a) Sally will turn ____________________ years old this Saturday.

b) I ____________________ hope all my friends can come to my party this weekend.

c) We live 1 ____________________ away from my grandma.

d) Marco caught a butterfly. He was sad when he had to ____________________ it.

e) Today, I have to ____________________ my project for the science fair.

f) My bedroom window has a nice ____________________ coming through today.

g) This striped caterpillar will ____________________ a monarch butterfly!

h) It will be a big ____________________ from the heat when the rain finally comes.

i) Rob has a ____________________ he will tell only to his best friend

j) Jackie didn't like her story, so she had to ____________________ it and start over.

Brain Stretch

How many spelling words can you fit into one sentence and still make sense? Give it a try!

Spelling Week 7 – Word Study

1. Unscramble the spelling word. Write the correct spelling on the line.

a) meboce ____________ b) ltcempoe ____________ c) lrfeie ____________

d) ctesre ____________ e) zrebee ____________ f) tefeifn ____________

g) leyral ____________ h) tkomlreie ____________ i) telede____________

2. Write as many letters and combinations of letters you can think of that have a long ***e*** sound.

____

____

3. Which provinces have a long ***e*** sound in their name? Write the names.

____

4. Compound words are two smaller words put together to make one bigger word. Draw a line between the two smaller words in the bigger word.

a) handmade	monkey	underwear	bicycle	sailboat
b) seastar	butter	about	doghouse	backyard
c) shadow	homework	binder	fingernail	rowboat
d) grouchy	thunder	eyelash	headache	skyline

Spelling Week 7 – Word Study

become	**breeze**	**complete**	**delete**	**fifteen**
kilometre	**really**	**relief**	**release**	**secret**

1. Write the correct spelling word from the list to match the clue.

a) A distance equal to 1000 metres ____________________

b) To remove or destroy ____________________

c) In actual fact; very or truly ____________________

d) Begin to be something ____________________

e) To let go, or set something free from captivity ____________________

f) To finish making or doing ____________________

g) A number less than 16 but more than 14 ____________________

h) A gentle wind ____________________

i) Something that is not to be known or seen by others ____________________

j) Feeling of reassurance and relaxation after release from stress or worry ____________________

2. Do **not** use the spelling word list for this activity. Write 2 words that have the long ***e*** sound made by the following letters:

a) ee ____________________ b) ie ____________________

c) y ____________________ d) ea ____________________

Spelling Week 8 – Words with a Long *i* Sound

Say each word out loud. Listen for the long ***i*** sound.

Copy and spell each word three times using colours of your choice.

1. crocodile ____________ ____________ ____________
2. beside ____________ ____________ ____________
3. inside ____________ ____________ ____________
4. awhile ____________ ____________ ____________
5. violin ____________ ____________ ____________
6. describe ____________ ____________ ____________
7. decide ____________ ____________ ____________
8. ninety ____________ ____________ ____________
9. fragile ____________ ____________ ____________
10. choir ____________ ____________ ____________

Spelling Tips: The long ***i*** sound can be spelled with

- letters ***igh*** and ***ign*** (*brighten, signed*)
- letter ***i*** followed by **consonant + *e*** (*smile*)
- letters ***ie*** and ***y*** (*lie, dry*)

Spelling Week 8 – Words with a Long *i* Sound

awhile	**beside**	**choir**	**crocodile**	**decide**
describe	**fragile**	**inside**	**ninety**	**violin**

1. Fill in the blank using the best spelling word from the list.

   a) We had a big birthday party when my grandma turned ____________________.

   b) Diane joined the ____________________ this year because she loves to sing.

   c) The teacher put an object on each desk and asked us to ____________________ it.

   d) The old teacups are very ____________________ and can break easily.

   e) A ____________________ and an alligator look similar, except for their snout shape.

   f) Just wait ____________________ and the dough will rise enough to bake the bread.

   g) Freddie had to ____________________ between an apple and a pear for a snack.

   h) If you look ____________________ any empty box in my house, you will find my cat.

   i) Carrie has ____________________ lessons every Saturday afternoon.

   j) Please set that book down ____________________ the box so I can pack it.

Brain Stretch

How many spelling words can you fit into one sentence and still make sense? Give it a try!

Spelling Week 8 – Word Study

1. Say the word out loud. Underline the words with the long ***i*** sound.

a) shine	ring	sigh	sky	tint
b) ship	flight	lazy	while	cry
c) tile	sign	grin	rhyme	bike
d) grime	fight	sick	lining	marry
e) spice	citizen	hair	dried	hire

2. A ***synonym*** is a word that means the same as another word.

Circle the synonym for the bolded word.

a) **shine** hurt gleam b) **sly** scared sneaky

3. Circle the word with the long ***i*** sound that makes the most sense.

Write the word in the sentence.

a) Han said he had to wait ______________ for the dentist today. (inside awhile)

b) The little glass figurine broke because it was ________________. (fragile ninety)

c) Grandad set his tea ______________ his sandwich. (beside inside)

d) I like to practice the _______________ on Monday nights. (choir violin)

e) Jim needs to _______________ the scarf he lost. (describe decide)

Spelling Week 8 – Word Study

1. Use the word list below to look for the words in the puzzle.

   Circle the word in the word search puzzle. Then cross out the word in the list.

C	R	Y	I	F	B	A	X	G
K	I	N	D	L	M	N	O	R
Y	K	P	E	I	O	O	Z	I
U	A	L	I	G	N	I	Y	N
H	W	I	N	H	N	S	O	D
E	H	F	Y	T	I	L	E	G
I	Y	E	T	F	G	D	F	E
G	X	A	C	O	H	L	I	H
H	Y	E	N	A	T	M	B	J
T	R	F	T	L	F	I	N	E

align **cry** **fine** **flight** **grind** **height**

hyena **kind** **life** **night** **tile** **why**

2. Write a word that rhymes with the word below. The word does not have to be spelled the same to rhyme.

   a) fine ______________ b) bike ______________ c) eye ______________

   d) pile ______________ e) try ______________ f) slide ______________

Spelling Week 9 – Words with a Long *o* Sound

Say each word out loud. Look at the different letters that make the long ***o*** sound.

Copy and spell each word three times using colours of your choice.

1. rodeo ______ ______ ______
2. pueblo ______ ______ ______
3. lower ______ ______ ______
4. trio ______ ______ ______
5. although ______ ______ ______
6. vocal ______ ______ ______
7. moment ______ ______ ______
8. poet ______ ______ ______
9. window ______ ______ ______
10. solo ______ ______ ______

Spelling Tips: A long ***o*** sound can be made with

- letter ***o*** (*troll, bonus, go*)
- letters ***oe*** (*toe*)
- letters ***oa*** and ***ow*** (*moat, crow*)
- letter ***o*** followed by a **consonant + *e*** (*mole*)

Spelling Week 9 – Words with a Long *o* Sound

although	**lower**	**moment**	**poet**	**pueblo**
rodeo	**solo**	**trio**	**vocal**	**window**

1. Fill in the blank using the best spelling word from the list.

   a) Teddy will sing a beautiful ____________________ at the next performance.

   b) A ____________________ is three of something.

   c) Some Native Americans live in a dried clay house called a ____________________.

   d) Sitting watching the sun set is a quiet ____________________ we always enjoy.

   e) ____________________ she was far away, she could still tell the spot was a spider.

   f) Mr. Smith next door rhymes very well. He's a very good ____________________.

   g) Aunt Judy takes her horse to the ____________________ to perform every summer!

   h) Sal's ____________________ coach is helping him learn to sing well.

   i) Trish had to set the rope ____________________ so she could grab onto it.

   j) A bird flew into our ____________________ this morning, but it wasn't hurt.

Brain Stretch

How many spelling words can you fit into one sentence and still make sense? Give it a try!

Spelling Week 9 – Word Study

1. Underline the words in the story that have a long ***o*** sound.

   Marco and his family took a trip to the zoo. Most of them were excited to see all the animals. But his cousin Lori didn't want to go. She was afraid of the hippos and polar bears. Her cousins Tony and Marco held her hand and told her about each animal as they went. There was so much to learn! When she saw the hippos rolling in the water, she started to laugh. The hippos were having fun! The polar bears were playing with a ball. They were having fun, too! One old bear was sleeping. Lori and her family were safe behind walls the whole time. When they left the zoo, Lori said she couldn't wait to go to the zoo again!

2. Circle the word with the long ***o*** sound that makes the most sense.

   Write the word in the sentence.

   a) Dave, Jim, and Ted sang together in a ______________. (solo trio)

   b) Kathy is training with her horse so they can be in a ________________. (rodeo pueblo)

   c) Aunt Irene teaches singing because she's a ______________ coach. (poet vocal)

   d) My cat Max likes to look out the _______________ to watch the birds. (window pueblo)

   e) The tree branch was too high, so we had to find a _______________ one. (solo lower)

3. An ***antonym*** is a word that has the opposite meaning of another word.

   Circle the antonym for the bolded word.

   a) **solo** five group b) **grow** stuck shrink

4. What does ***growing*** mean in the sentence? Circle the correct definition.

   Maxine is really growing as a writer.

   developing and increasing in ability increasing in size and maturity

Spelling Week 9 – Word Study

although	**lower**	**moment**	**poet**	**pueblo**
rodeo	**solo**	**trio**	**vocal**	**window**

1. Write the correct spelling word from the list to match the clue.

a) Farther down than something else ____________________

b) A Native American house made of red, sun-baked clay ____________________

c) An event where cowboys and cowgirls compete and perform to show their agility and skill on horseback ____________________

d) Someone who writes poems ____________________

e) Done by one person alone ____________________

f) An opening in a wall that is fitted with framed glass ____________________

g) About or relating to one's voice ____________________

h) A group of three ____________________

i) Even though; however ____________________

j) A very brief or important period of time ____________________

2. Do <u>**not**</u> use the spelling word list for this activity. Write 2 words that have the long ***o*** sound made by the following letters:

a) oe ______________________________ b) oa ______________________________

c) ow ______________________________ d) o ______________________________

Spelling Week 10 – Words with a Long *u* Sound

Say each word out loud. Look at the different letters that make the long ***u*** sound.

Copy and spell each word three times using colours of your choice.

1. bugle __________ __________ __________
2. jewel __________ __________ __________
3. university __________ __________ __________
4. commute __________ __________ __________
5. amuse __________ __________ __________
6. pupil __________ __________ __________
7. askew __________ __________ __________
8. computer __________ __________ __________
9. utensil __________ __________ __________
10. acute __________ __________ __________

Spelling Tips: A long ***u*** sound can be made with

- letter ***u*** followed by a **consonant + *e*** (*reuse*)
- letter ***u*** followed by a **consonant + *i*** or ***y*** (*cupid, jury*)
- letters ***ue*** (*cue*)
- letters ***ew*** (*few, ewe*)

Spelling Week 10 – Words with a Long *u* Sound

acute	**amuse**	**askew**	**bugle**	**commute**
computer	**jewel**	**pupil**	**university**	**utensil**

1. Fill in the blank using the best spelling word from the list.

   a) I bumped the frame as I walked past. Now the painting is ____________________.

   b) The queen had a huge blue ____________________ on her crown.

   c) When a bird gets angry, the ____________________ in its eye gets smaller.

   d) My cousin Jake will go to ____________________ to become a doctor.

   e) A spoon is the best ____________________ to use when you're eating soup.

   f) Pat lives far out of town, so she has to ____________________ to her job every day.

   g) Our kitten rolls a toy mouse around to ____________________ herself.

   h) My ____________________ helps me go on the Internet to research topics.

   i) My grandfather played the ____________________ in the army.

   j) An angle that measures less than 90° is called an ____________________ angle.

Brain Stretch

How many spelling words can you fit into one sentence and still make sense? Give it a try!

Spelling Week 10 – Word Study

Long vowels say their name! So when you say words with long vowels, you hear the letter names ***A*** (game), ***E*** (team), ***I*** (bite), ***O*** (goat), and ***U*** (use).

The long ***u*** should sound just like the word ***you***. For example, the word ***June*** sounds like ***Jyoune***. Other letter combinations, such as ***ew***, ***ue***, and a ***consonant + e***, ***i***, or ***y***, can also make the long ***u*** sound. However, all of those letters, including ***u*** itself, can also make other sounds that do not sound like the word ***you***.

1. Say the word out loud. Listen for sounds the letters make. Underline the words that have the long ***u*** sound.

a) rescue	due	cute	flu	unit
b) true	university	blew	menu	yule
c) clue	music	argue	flew	cue
d) few	view	blue	unite	grew

2. The word ***pupil*** can have two meanings.
   Write a sentence to show each meaning of the word ***pupil***.

   ____

   ____

3. Write a sentence using the word ***unique***.

   ____

Spelling Week 10 – Word Study

1. Use the word list below to look for the words in the puzzle.

   Circle the word in the word search puzzle. Then cross out the word in the list.

U	N	I	C	O	R	N	X	A
N	E	I	D	L	M	N	O	R
I	R	C	E	C	O	O	Z	G
Q	C	U	E	F	I	C	Y	U
U	W	P	F	A	J	U	N	E
E	U	I	E	S	T	Z	R	G
V	N	D	W	F	K	E	W	E
O	I	Y	E	W	T	L	I	H
I	T	L	R	E	U	S	E	J
R	E	S	C	U	E	U	G	Z

argue	**cue**	**cupid**	**ewe**	**few**	**June**
rescue	**reuse**	**unicorn**	**unique**	**unit**	**yew**

2. Just for fun, let's look at some other letter combinations and words that have a long ***u*** sound. The letter combinations include ***oo***, ***oe***, ***ui***, and ***ugh***. Say the words out loud. Use the pronunciation key to pronounce any words you don't know.

shoo and shoe [shyou]	manual [man-you-ull]	Hugh [hyou]
juice [jyouss]	ukulele [you-kuh-lay-lee]	ewe [you]

Spelling Week 11 – Words with *y* as Long *i* and Long *e* Sounds

Say each word out loud. Listen for the long ***i*** and long ***e*** sounds.

Copy and spell each word three times using colours of your choice.

1. dirty __________ __________ __________
2. comedy __________ __________ __________
3. bytes __________ __________ __________
4. parsley __________ __________ __________
5. type __________ __________ __________
6. anyone __________ __________ __________
7. recycle __________ __________ __________
8. monkey __________ __________ __________
9. reply __________ __________ __________
10. merely __________ __________ __________

Brain Stretch

- Create a word search puzzle based on the spelling words.
- On a piece of paper, write a sentence using each spelling word.

Spelling Week 11 – Words with *y* as Long *i* and Long *e* Sounds

anyone	**bytes**	**comedy**	**dirty**	**merely**
monkey	**parsley**	**recycle**	**reply**	**type**

1. Fill in the blank using the best spelling word from the list.

   a) I love ____________________ movies! What's your favourite kind of movie?

   b) After planting the little tree, Maggie's hands were all ____________________.

   c) Grandma sent me a letter. I am going to ____________________ to it today.

   d) A ____________________ at the zoo needed a name, so we named him Jupiter.

   e) All computer files take up space in units called ____________________.

   f) She didn't plan to adopt a dog. She was ____________________ looking at them.

   g) You should always ____________________ as much waste as possible.

   h) I ____________________ my reports on the laptop at school.

   i) Mom grows fresh ____________________ in the kitchen to use in cooking.

   j) Jay asked, "Does ____________________ want another slice of pizza?"

Brain Stretch

How many spelling words can you fit into one sentence and still make sense? Give it a try!

Spelling Week 11 – Word Study

1. Read the sentence clue. Unscramble the word and write it in the space.

   a) Dad's favourite show is a ___________ about two men and a baby. (dmecoy)

   b) I don't know _______________ who doesn't like vanilla ice cream. (oynaen)

   c) _______________ tastes good on fried fish. (lprsaey)

   d) The zookeeper gave a bunch of bananas to the _______________. (ynomke)

   e) We have a blue _______________ bin in our classroom. (crycele)

   f) Our dog likes to play in the mud, so she is often very ___________. (rydit)

2. Circle the compound words. Write the two words that make the word with a + sign.

   Example: *doghouse* *dog + house*

   a) eyeball deny fly daydream crayon

   ____

   b) cherry anyone monkey apply bodyguard

   ____

   c) delay blueberry berry firefly afraid

   ____

Spelling Week 11 – Word Study

anyone	**bytes**	**comedy**	**dirty**	**merely**
monkey	**parsley**	**recycle**	**reply**	**type**

1. Write the correct spelling word from the list to match the clue.

   a) To convert waste into reusable material ________________

   b) A unit of computer information ________________

   c) A small- to medium-sized long-tailed primate which lives in trees in tropical countries ________________

   d) Not clean ________________

   e) A show, book, or movie that is funny ________________

   f) Nothing more than ________________

   g) To use a keyboard to write on a computer ________________

   h) A scented green plant used in cooking ________________

   i) Any person or any people ________________

   j) Say something in response to something that was said ________________

2. The word ***type*** can have two meanings. Write a sentence to show each meaning.

____

____

Spelling Week 12 – Contractions

Say each word out loud. Think about what letter or letters are missing.

Copy and spell each word three times using colours of your choice.

1. isn't ______ ______ ______
2. he's ______ ______ ______
3. you'll ______ ______ ______
4. can't ______ ______ ______
5. don't ______ ______ ______
6. they're ______ ______ ______
7. haven't ______ ______ ______
8. we're ______ ______ ______
9. couldn't ______ ______ ______
10. she's ______ ______ ______

Brain Stretch

- Create a word search puzzle based on the spelling words.
- On a piece of paper, write a sentence using each spelling word.

Spelling Week 12 – Contractions

can't	**don't**	**haven't**	**he's**	**isn't**
she's	**they're**	**we're**	**wouldn't**	**you'll**

1. Fill in the blank using the best spelling word from the list.

a) Cam and Ali have told me ____________________ coming to my party.

b) Trish's baby brother ____________________ stand by himself yet.

c) ____________________ all going to the library this afternoon.

d) That blue top ____________________ the one I was looking for.

e) Jimmy said ____________________ helping his dad build a birdhouse.

f) I think ____________________ be surprised to see how much our puppy has grown.

g) Katy told me ____________________ baking a cake for her mother's birthday.

h) My project is due tomorrow but I ____________________ finished it yet.

i) Sam thought he ____________________ like to eat tacos, but he does.

j) "____________________ that your brother over there?" asked Kim.

Brain Stretch

How many spelling words can you fit into one sentence and still make sense? Give it a try!

Spelling Week 12 – Word Study

There are two tricky contractions. You will have to learn these contractions.

will not = ***won't*** ***cannot*** = ***can't***

1. Circle the incorrect contraction.
   Write the correct contraction at the end of the sentence.

   a) Eddie willn't be coming to my party this weekend. ______________

   b) I cann't wait for the weekend to get here! ______________

   c) Sara wil'nt tell Mary's secret to anyone. ______________

   d) Jay cant see clearly without his glasses. ______________

   e) Donot you want to swim with us tomorrow? ______________

   f) Hasnot she seen this movie before? ______________

2. Read the contraction. Write the words in full.

   Example: I'm I am

a) couldn't ________________	b) hadn't ________________
c) we've ________________	d) she's ________________
e) that's ________________	f) can't ________________
g) isn't ________________	h) won't ________________
i) you're ________________	j) didn't ________________

1. You are going to decode a secret message! The letters of the alphabet are each represented by a number, as shown below.

1	2	3	4	5	6	7	8	9	10	11	12	13
A	**B**	**C**	**D**	**E**	**F**	**G**	**H**	**I**	**J**	**K**	**L**	**M**

14	15	16	17	18	19	20	21	22	23	24	25	26
N	**O**	**P**	**Q**	**R**	**S**	**T**	**U**	**V**	**W**	**X**	**Y**	**Z**

Write the letter on the line above the number to decode the message.

a)

___ ’ ___ ___ / ___ ___ ___ / ___ ___ ___ ___ / ___ ___ ___ / ___ ___ ___ ___
9 20 19   14 15 20   23 8 1 20   25 15 21   12 15 15 11

___ ___ / ___ ___ ___ ___ / ___ ___ ___ ___ ___ ___ ___ , / ___ ’ ___ ___
1 20   20 8 1 20   13 1 20 20 5 18 19   9 20 19

___ ___ ___ ___ / ___ ___ ___ / ___ ___ ___ .
23 8 1 20   25 15 21   19 5 5

b)

___ ___ ___ ’ ___ / ___ ___ / ___ ___ ___ ___ ___ ___ ___ / ___ ___ ___ / ___
9 19 14 20   9 20   1 13 1 26 9 14 7   8 15 23   1

___ ___ ___ ___ ___ ___ / ___ ___ ___ / ___ ___ ___ / ___ ___ ___ ___ / ___
16 5 18 19 15 14   23 8 15   23 1 19   15 14 3 5   1

___ ___ ___ ___ ___ ___ ___ ___ / ___ ___ ___ / ___ ___ ___ ___ ___ ___ ___ ___
19 20 18 1 14 7 5 18   3 1 14   19 21 4 4 5 14 12 25

___ ___ ___ ___ ___ ___ / ___ ___ ___ ___ / ___ ___ ___ ___ / ___ ___ ___ ___ ___ ___ ?
2 5 3 15 13 5   25 15 21 18   2 5 19 20   6 18 9 5 14 4

Spelling Week 13 – Double Consonants

Say each word out loud. Watch for the double consonants.

Copy and spell each word three times using colours of your choice.

1. cotton __________ __________ __________
2. tossed __________ __________ __________
3. actress __________ __________ __________
4. occasion __________ __________ __________
5. drill __________ __________ __________
6. puzzle __________ __________ __________
7. luggage __________ __________ __________
8. afford __________ __________ __________
9. hammer __________ __________ __________
10. barrel __________ __________ __________

Brain Stretch

- Create a word search puzzle based on the spelling words.
- On a piece of paper, write a sentence using each spelling word.

Spelling Week 13 – Double Consonants

actress	**afford**	**barrel**	**cotton**	**drill**
hammer	**luggage**	**occasion**	**puzzle**	**tossed**

1. Fill in the blank using the best spelling word from the list.

    a) When my grandmother goes on vacation, she takes a lot of ____________________.

    b) Ani wants to be an ____________________ when she grows up.

    c) Matt and Han ____________________ a ball around in the backyard.

    d) Mrs. Henry grows pansies in a big wooden ____________________ in her yard.

    e) Jimmy and Amy are putting together an animal jigsaw ____________________.

    f) I saved my allowance all year to be able to ____________________ to buy a bike.

    g) Mom had to ____________________ holes in the wall to put the mirror up.

    h) Grandma stuffed my doll with ____________________ to make her soft.

    i) Dad needs to buy a ____________________ so he can fix the boards on the deck.

    j) Whenever a special ____________________ comes up, Kerry curls her hair.

Brain Stretch

How many spelling words can you fit into one sentence and still make sense? Give it a try!

Spelling Week 13 – Word Study

For many verbs that end with **consonant + vowel + consonant**, double the final consonant before adding ***ed*** or ***ing***.

Examples:	**Verb**	**Add ed**	**Add ing**
	tan	*tanned*	*tanning*
	clap	*clapped*	*clapping*

1. Add ***ed*** and ***ing*** to the verb. Remember to double the final consonant when needed.

a) spell ____________________ ____________________

b) knit ____________________ ____________________

c) toss ____________________ ____________________

d) plan ____________________ ____________________

e) walk ____________________ ____________________

2. Put a ✔ beside the word if it is spelled correctly. If the word is spelled incorrectly, put an **X** beside the word and write the word correctly.

a) foldding ____________________ b) missed ____________________

c) tripped ____________________ d) mashhing ____________________

e) spilled ____________________ f) meltting ____________________

g) laughed ____________________ h) talkking ____________________

Spelling Week 13 – Word Study

1. Use the word list below to look for the words in the puzzle.

Circle the word in the word search puzzle. Then cross out the word in the list.

S	N	U	G	G	L	E	T	M
D	O	L	L	A	R	M	U	U
C	U	P	P	E	R	A	G	F
U	S	H	O	P	Z	T	G	F
D	B	T	H	W	O	T	E	I
D	U	F	Y	S	T	E	D	N
L	B	U	K	N	P	R	F	E
E	B	Z	B	U	Z	Z	E	R
I	L	Z	T	A	L	L	E	R
D	E	Y	P	U	P	P	Y	Z

bubble	**buzzer**	**cuddle**	**dollar**	**fuzzy**	**matter**
muffin	**puppy**	**snuggle**	**taller**	**tugged**	**upper**

2. Write a word that rhymes with the word below. The words do not have to be spelled the same.

a) will ________________ b) setter ________________ c) miller ________________

d) batter ________________ e) moss ________________ f) penny ________________

g) funny________________ h) bell ________________ i) hall ________________

Spelling Week 14 – Words with Silent Letters

Say each word out loud. Listen for which letters you don't hear.

Copy and spell each word three times using colours of your choice.

1. sketch ____________ ____________ ____________
2. calf ____________ ____________ ____________
3. guest ____________ ____________ ____________
4. castle ____________ ____________ ____________
5. listening ____________ ____________ ____________
6. whisper ____________ ____________ ____________
7. chords ____________ ____________ ____________
8. wrench ____________ ____________ ____________
9. orange ____________ ____________ ____________
10. weigh ____________ ____________ ____________

Spelling Tip

For many words that end in a vowel followed by a **consonant + silent e**, the ***e*** makes the vowel say its name.

Spelling Week 14 – Words with Silent Letters

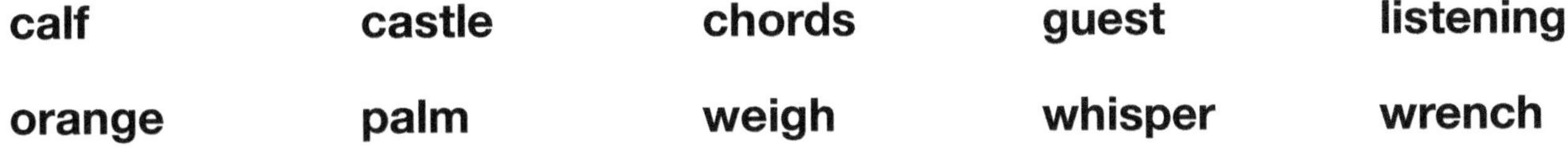

calf	**castle**	**chords**	**guest**	**listening**
orange	**palm**	**weigh**	**whisper**	**wrench**

1. Fill in the blank using the best spelling word from the list.

a) I'm learning to play the ____________________ on my guitar.

b) Tammy is wearing ____________________ shorts, a pink top, and green socks.

c) Coconuts and dates grow on two different types of ____________________ trees.

d) We have to talk in a ____________________ so we don't wake my baby sister.

e) Ari and Bill are ____________________ to the country music station.

f) Uncle Jeff's cow Bessie has a new spotted ____________________.

g) Mom said we'll be having a ____________________ over for dinner. I wonder who?

h) The plumber used a very large ____________________ to take the pipe off.

i) Sally explored the ruins of an old ____________________ high on a hilltop.

j) The grocer has to ____________________ these fruits and vegetables for us.

Brain Stretch

How many spelling words can you fit into one sentence and still make sense? Give it a try!

Spelling Week 14 – Word Study

1. Say the word out loud. Can you hear all the letter sounds? Circle words with silent letters. Underline the silent letters.

a) bright	cube	swoop	flu	honest
b) wheel	unique	blew	menu	yule
c) school	lump	argue	flew	walk
d) boots	view	blue	night	listen
e) half	nag	crumb	took	gnome

2. Say the word out loud. Add **e** to the end of the word. Write the new word. Say the word again.

	Add *e*		Add *e*
a) car		b) spin	
c) kit		d) cut	
e) not		f) scrap	
g) mad		h) dim	

3. What happens to the vowel when you add **e** to the end of the word?

____

4. Write the number words from one to ten that end in silent ***e***.

____

5. For each number word in Question 4, write a word that rhymes with it.

____

Spelling Week 14 – Word Study

calf	castle	chords	guest	listening
orange	palm	weigh	whisper	wrench

1. Write the correct spelling word from the list to match the clue.

   a) A type of tropical tree or the front of a human hand ____________________

   b) Giving one's attention to a sound or person speaking ____________________

   c) A group of three or more notes played at the same time to create a harmony ____________________

   d) A baby cow ____________________

   e) To speak very quietly ____________________

   f) The building where a king or queen lived long ago ____________________

   g) A person who is invited to visit a home or take part in a function that was organized by someone else ____________________

   h) A tool used to loosen pipes and nuts ____________________

   i) Find out how heavy something is ____________________

   j) A sweet, round citrus fruit that is often made into juice ____________________

2. Do **not** use the spelling word list for this activity. Write a word that has the following silent letters:

   a) wr ____________________ b) gh ____________________

   c) b ____________________ d) t ____________________

Spelling Week 15 – Words with Long and Short *oo* Sounds

Say each word out loud. Look at the different letters that makethe long and short ***oo*** sounds.

Copy and spell each word three times using colours of your choice.

1. crooked ____________ ____________ ____________
2. stood ____________ ____________ ____________
3. aloof ____________ ____________ ____________
4. loom ____________ ____________ ____________
5. mistook ____________ ____________ ____________
6. grew ____________ ____________ ____________
7. brook ____________ ____________ ____________
8. tomb ____________ ____________ ____________
9. bamboo ____________ ____________ ____________
10. would ____________ ____________ ____________

Spelling Tips

The long ***oo*** sound can be spelled with

- letters ***ew*** (*blew*) and ***ue*** (*glue*)
- letters ***oo*** (*soon*)
- letters ***ough*** (*through*)

The short ***oo*** sound can be spelled with

- letters ***oo*** (*wood*)
- letters ***ou*** (*should*)

Spelling Week 15 – Words with Long and Short *oo* Sounds

aloof	**bamboo**	**brook**	**crooked**	**grew**
loom	**mistook**	**stood**	**tomb**	**would**

1. Fill in the blank using the best spelling word from the list.

   a) My teeth were all ________________ so I got braces to straighten them.

   b) The giant panda lives in the jungle and eats ________________.

   c) My Aunt Peggy weaves rugs on a big ________________.

   d) We watched minnows swimming in the little ________________ near our house.

   e) The maple key I planted eight years ago ________________ into a tall tree.

   f) Cats mostly act very ________________ unless they want something from you.

   g) Our neighbour ________________ me for my brother today.

   h) An owl statue ________________ in the middle of that garden last year.

   i) King Tut had a lot of golden objects in his ________________.

   j) Sometimes, I think I ________________ like to be an animal for a few days.

Brain Stretch

How many spelling words can you fit into one sentence and still make sense? Give it a try!

Spelling Week 15 – Word Study

1. Circle the words that have a long ***oo*** sound. Some of the words have the same sound but are spelled differently.

a) good	tuna	though	blew	true
b) glue	crew	shoulder	loud	fruit
c) pool	bump	loose	sour	due
d) books	review	soup	loom	enough

2. Circle the words that have a short ***oo*** sound. Some of the words have the same sound but are spelled differently.

a) stood	cold	could	flu	look
b) whole	soot	grew	should	woof
c) hood	loose	wood	flew	pull
d) boots	view	cookie	brook	foot

3. Write the correct letter beside the word. Write ***S*** for a short ***oo*** sound, ***L*** for a long ***oo*** sound, and ***N*** for neither sound.

a) crook ______	b) puff ______	c) moon ______
d) poof ______	e) brown ______	f) would ______
g) sponge ______	h) crook ______	i) glue ______

Spelling Week 15 – Word Study

1. Use the word list below to look for the words in the puzzle.

   Circle the word in the word search puzzle. Then cross out the word in the list.

C	O	O	K	I	E	F	N	A
S	H	O	O	K	M	L	C	V
P	U	L	L	C	S	U	O	X
O	K	H	C	F	I	T	U	B
O	M	O	O	D	V	E	L	L
L	H	O	Y	S	T	E	D	O
V	Q	D	T	F	G	D	F	O
O	Y	A	C	R	E	W	I	M
S	U	I	T	I	K	M	B	J
D	R	F	W	O	U	L	D	Z

bloom	**cookie**	**could**	**crew**	**flute**	**hood**
mood	**pull**	**shook**	**spool**	**suit**	**would**

2. Write a word that rhymes with the word below. Rhyming words do not have to be spelled in the same way.

a) root ______________ b) crook ______________ c) noon ______________

d) doom ______________ e) full ______________ f) grew ______________

g) drool ______________ h) wood ______________ i) moose ______________

Spelling Week 16 – Words with *oi* and *oy*

Say each word out loud. Listen to the sounds ***oi*** and **oy** make.

Copy and spell each word three times using colours of your choice.

1. destroy __________ __________ __________
2. decoy __________ __________ __________
3. avoid __________ __________ __________
4. poison __________ __________ __________
5. loyal __________ __________ __________
6. oyster __________ __________ __________
7. choice __________ __________ __________
8. moisture __________ __________ __________
9. voyage __________ __________ __________
10. joined __________ __________ __________

Brain Stretch

- Create a word search puzzle based on the spelling words.
- On a piece of paper, write a sentence using each spelling word.

Spelling Week 16 – Words with *oi* and *oy*

avoid	**choice**	**decoy**	**destroy**	**joined**
loyal	**moisture**	**oyster**	**poison**	**voyage**

1. Fill in the blank using the best spelling word from the list.

   a) I accidentally walked through ___________________ ivy and now my legs are itchy.

   b) My grandfather said he once opened an ___________________ and found a pearl.

   c) Our teacher gave us the ___________________ of painting or making a collage.

   d) The tent caterpillars in our tree will ___________________ the leaves on that branch.

   e) Captain Cook went on a ___________________ from England to North America.

   f) My aunt's dog Tank is a very ___________________ companion for her.

   g) When Dad takes a shower, ___________________ collects on the bathroom mirror.

   h) I try to ___________________ the corner house because their dog barks at me.

   i) Uncle Jeff carves and paints ___________________ ducks to sell.

   j) At school, I ___________________ the band and the drama club.

Brain Stretch

How many spelling words can you fit into one sentence and still make sense? Give it a try!

Spelling Week 16 – Word Study

1. Read the sentence clue. Unscramble the word and write it in the space.

   a) When my best friend Karen is mad at me, she tries hard to ____________ me. (dovia)

   b) In Japan, they raise ________________ to get pearls from them. (tsoreys)

   c) Treat your pets with kindness and they'll become ________________ friends. (yloal)

   d) In class, our group ________________ with another group to work on a project. (ejinod)

   e) There are many ________________ mushrooms in the forest. (sopion)

   f) We're going on a long ocean ________________ next month. (yvgaeo)

2. Circle the compound words. Write the two words that make the word with a **+** sign.

   Example: *doghouse* *dog + house*

   a) strawberry rely kitten bathtub dragon

   ____

   b) berries campfire donkey honest cheesecake

   ____

   c) farming doughnut merry playground elephant

   ____

Spelling Week 16 – Word Study

avoid	**choice**	**decoy**	**destroy**	**joined**
loyal	**moisture**	**oyster**	**poison**	**voyage**

1. Write the correct spelling word from the list to match the clue.

   a) A substance that can cause illness or death ____________________

   b) A mollusc that has a rough shell and can produce pearls ____________________

   c) An imitation bird or animal used by hunters to attract other birds or animals ____________________

   d) Became linked or connected to ____________________

   e) To keep away from or stop oneself from doing something ____________________

   f) A long journey by sea or in space ____________________

   g) The act of selecting or make a decision when faced with two or more possibilities ____________________

   h) To put an end to the existence of something ____________________

   i) Able to give or show firm and constant support ____________________

   j) Water or other liquid spread as a vapour, within a solid, or condensed on a surface ____________________

2. Do **<u>not</u>** use the spelling word list for this activity. Write two words that contain the following letters:

   a) oi ____

   b) oy ____

Spelling Week 17 – Words with an *ow* Sound: *ou* and *ow*

Say each word out loud. Listen for the ***ow*** sound.

Copy and spell each word three times using colours of your choice.

1. frown __________ __________ __________
2. browser __________ __________ __________
3. count __________ __________ __________
4. mountain __________ __________ __________
5. brown __________ __________ __________
6. crowd __________ __________ __________
7. pounce __________ __________ __________
8. council __________ __________ __________
9. towel __________ __________ __________
10. couch __________ __________ __________

Brain Stretch

- Create a word search puzzle based on the spelling words.
- On a piece of paper, write a sentence using each spelling word.

Spelling Week 17 – Words with an *ow* Sound: *ou* and *ow*

brown	**browser**	**council**	**couch**	**count**
crowd	**frown**	**mountain**	**pounce**	**towel**

1. Fill in the blank using the best spelling word from the list.

   a) We've had no rain for so long that the grass has all turned ____________________.

   b) A ____________________ of people gathered to watch the juggler in the park.

   c) On Friday, I learned to ____________________ all the money in my piggy bank.

   d) That cat is getting ready to ____________________ on a grasshopper.

   e) My goal is to one day climb to the top of that ____________________.

   f) Helga accidentally dropped her beach ____________________ in the mud.

   g) Our dog's markings make him look like he has a constant ____________________.

   h) We use the DuckDuckGo ____________________ to navigate the Internet at school.

   i) Our neighbour Ted is a member of the town ____________________.

   j) My aunt's dog Bruno is lying on our ____________________ waiting for belly rubs.

Brain Stretch

How many spelling words can you fit into one sentence and still make sense? Give it a try!

Spelling Week 17 – Word Study

1. The letters ***ou*** and ***ow*** can have an ***ow*** sound or an ***o*** sound. Say the word out loud. Underline the words that have an ***ow*** sound. Circle the words that have an ***o*** sound.

a) grow	proud	though	allow	know
b) sprout	marshmallow	loud	below	ground
c) grouch	narrow	fowl	snow	shadow
d) bounce	throw	cloud	scout	pillow

2. ***Homophones*** are words that sound the same, but are spelled differently and have different meanings. Say the word out loud. Draw a line from the word to its meaning.

a) read	painful and aching
b) reed	story
c) soar	propelled something through the air with force
d) sore	tall, thin grass-like aquatic plant
e) tail	official chair a king or queen sits on
f) tale	see and take in the meaning of letters and symbols
g) thrown	fly or rise high in the air
h) throne	end part of an animal

Spelling Week 17 – Word Study

1. Use the word list below to look for the words in the puzzle.

   Circle the word in the word search puzzle. Then cross out the word in the list.

F	O	U	N	T	A	I	N	S
E	B	I	G	R	O	U	C	H
L	O	W	E	R	O	O	Z	A
L	R	J	S	F	I	I	Y	L
O	R	C	N	Q	A	T	S	L
W	O	M	O	U	T	H	C	O
V	W	Y	W	F	G	F	O	W
O	Y	A	C	O	L	L	U	H
P	O	U	T	I	O	M	R	J
N	A	R	R	O	W	U	G	Z

borrow **fellow** **fountain** **glow** **grouch** **lower**

mouth **narrow** **pout** **scour** **snow** **shallow**

2. Write a word that ends in the same letters that are underlined below.

   Examples: ***pout*** ***scout*** ***gown*** ***town*** ***count*** ***mount***

a) pouch ______________ b) brown ______________ c) scour ______________

d) scowl ______________ e) pound ______________ f) power ______________

g) south ______________ h) loud ______________ i) house ______________

Spelling Week 18 – Words with an *s* Sound: *c* and *s*

Say each word out loud. Look at the different letters that make an **s** sound.

Copy and spell each word three times using colours of your choice.

1. prince ____________ ____________ ____________
2. request ____________ ____________ ____________
3. minus ____________ ____________ ____________
4. space ____________ ____________ ____________
5. passage ____________ ____________ ____________
6. thirsty ____________ ____________ ____________
7. obtuse ____________ ____________ ____________
8. switch ____________ ____________ ____________
9. whistle ____________ ____________ ____________
10. tinsel ____________ ____________ ____________

Spelling Tip

The ***s*** sound can be spelled with the letters ***s***, ***ce***, ***ci***, and ***cy***.

minus	**obtuse**	**passage**	**prince**	**request**
space	**switch**	**thirsty**	**tinsel**	**whistle**

1. Fill in the blank using the best spelling word from the list.

   a) There's a cat sleeping in the ____________________ between those buildings.

   b) The hallway has a light ____________________ at each end.

   c) Mom put out a fresh bowl of water because our dog is ____________________.

   d) Sam is trying to figure out the answer for 20 ____________________ 6.

   e) My Uncle Tony can ____________________ very loudly to call his dog.

   f) In geometry, a 120° angle is called an ____________________ angle.

   g) If you have a cat, you shouldn't use ____________________ on your Christmas tree.

   h) In fairy tales, the handsome ____________________ always rescues the princess.

   i) There is a large ____________________ in the fence where the dog sneaks through.

   j) Zack is going to ____________________ a new book for the library to bring in.

Brain Stretch

How many spelling words can you fit into one sentence and still make sense? Give it a try!

Spelling Week 18 – Word Study

1. Say the word out loud. Circle the words that do **not** have an ***s*** sound.

a) glance	organism	pastel	piece	reason
b) icicle	fleece	browser	receive	pause
c) crush	clothes	mercy	cookies	canvas
d) bicycle	claws	recite	present	since

2. ***Homographs*** are words that are spelled the same, but have different meanings and can sometimes sound different. Read the pronunciation key if there is one. Draw a line from the word to its meaning. You can use a dictionary, if needed.

a) bat	tall bird with long legs and a long neck
b) bat	drop of salty liquid from a human's eye
c) lead [lehd]	wooden or metal object used to hit a ball
d) lead [leed]	rip apart
e) crane	soft, heavy grey metal
f) crane	winged noctural animal that eats insects
g) tear [teer]	show the way or guide someone to a place
h) tear [tayr]	tall machine used to pick up and move large or heavy objects on a construction site

Spelling Week 18 – Word Study

1. Use the word list below to look for the words in the puzzle.

Circle the word in the word search puzzle. Then cross out the word in the list.

W	S	T	E	N	C	I	L	A
H	P	R	E	C	I	P	E	J
I	E	G	L	A	N	C	E	U
S	A	U	C	E	I	I	Y	I
T	C	R	I	G	S	B	O	C
L	E	O	T	F	T	R	R	Y
E	Q	P	Y	A	G	A	F	E
O	Y	X	P	N	I	S	I	H
T	C	I	R	C	U	S	B	J
S	P	I	C	Y	H	Q	G	Z

brass	**circus**	**city**	**fancy**	**glance**	**juicy**
peace	**recipe**	**sauce**	**spicy**	**stencil**	**whistle**

2. Write a word that rhymes with the word below. The word can be spelled differently.

a) sift ____________ b) rice ____________ c) chance ____________

d) list ____________ e) pace ____________ f) less ____________

g) west ____________ h) juice ____________ i) cider ____________

Spelling Week 19 – Words with a *j* Sound: *g* and *j*

Say each word out loud. Look at the different letters that make a *j* sound.

Copy and spell each word three times using colours of your choice.

1. fragile ______ ______ ______
2. jewel ______ ______ ______
3. engineer ______ ______ ______
4. bridge ______ ______ ______
5. juggle ______ ______ ______
6. ecology ______ ______ ______
7. gerbil ______ ______ ______
8. region ______ ______ ______
9. energy ______ ______ ______
10. reject ______ ______ ______

Spelling Tip

The *j* sound can be spelled with the letters ***j***, ***ge***, ***gy***, and ***gi***.

Spelling Week 19 – Words with a *j* Sound: *g* and *j*

bridge	**ecology**	**energy**	**engineer**	**fragile**
gerbil	**jewel**	**juggle**	**region**	**reject**

1. Fill in the blank using the best spelling word from the list.

a) Sometimes, the gumball machine will ____________________ my quarter.

b) The tiny glass animals on my grandma's dresser are very ____________________.

c) We drive across a big wooden ____________________ on the way to our cottage.

d) My aunt and uncle live in the mountain ____________________ in British Columbia.

e) Timmy got a new pet ____________________ on his birthday.

f) ____________________ is the study of plants, animals, and their environments.

g) My mother can sometimes ____________________ three objects at once.

h) Eating the right foods gives you enough ____________________ to work and play.

i) The king's crown had a big red ____________________ on the front.

j) I want to be a space ____________________ when I grow up.

Brain Stretch

How many spelling words can you fit into one sentence and still make sense? Give it a try!

Spelling Week 19 – Word Study

1. Say the word out loud. Circle the words that do **not** have a ***j*** sound.

a) angry	angel	girl	jacks	giant
b) injury	gymnasium	organize	pigeon	giggle
c) gear	janitor	gift	fridge	ginger
d) magic	geese	piggy	range	finger

2. The letters "ology" mean "the study of." When these letters are added to the end of a word, the beginning of the word tells what is being studied. Use a dictionary or the Internet to find the word meaning. Write a brief definition beside the word.

Example: zoology   the study of animals, their bodies, and their behaviour

a) criminology ____

b) geology ____

c) paleontology ____

d) meteorology ____

e) volcanology ____

f) ornithology ____

g) herpetology ____

h) dermatology ____

Spelling Week 19 – Word Study

bridge	**ecology**	**energy**	**engineer**	**fragile**
gerbil	**jewel**	**juggle**	**region**	**reject**

1. Write the correct spelling word from the list to match the clue.

a) A cut and polished precious stone ____________________

b) Available power, or the ability to do work or be active ____________________

c) To continually toss and catch a number of objects, keeping at least one in the air at all times ____________________

d) Structure built over something so people can cross ____________________

e) Mouse-like rodent adapted to living in desert conditions ____________________

f) Easy to damage or break ____________________

g) A person who designs, builds, or maintains engines, machines, or public works such as bridges and roads ____________________

h) The study of plants and animals, and their environments ____________________

i) An area or division, especially of a country or the world ____________________

j) To refuse to accept, use, or believe something or someone ____________________

2. Do **<u>not</u>** use the spelling word list for this activity. Write a word that has the ***j*** sound made by the following letters. These letters can be anywhere in the word.

a) j ____________________ b) ge ____________________

c) gi ____________________ d) gy ____________________

Spelling Week 20 – Words with an *f* Sound: ***ph, gh,*** and ***f***

Say each word out loud. Listen to the ***f*** sound the different letters make.

Copy and spell each word three times using colours of your choice.

1. rough ________ ________ ________
2. enough ________ ________ ________
3. amphibian ________ ________ ________
4. half ________ ________ ________
5. elephant ________ ________ ________
6. tough ________ ________ ________
7. surface ________ ________ ________
8. orphan ________ ________ ________
9. inflate ________ ________ ________
10. offer ________ ________ ________

Brain Stretch

- Create a word search puzzle based on the spelling words.
- On a piece of paper, write a sentence using each spelling word.

Spelling Week 20 – Words with an *f* Sound: ***ph, gh,*** and ***f***

amphibian	**elephant**	**enough**	**half**	**inflate**
offer	**orphan**	**rough**	**surface**	**tough**

1. Fill in the blank using the best spelling word from the list.

   a) Spending 15 minutes outside on a very hot day is ________________ for me.

   b) Dad used a bicycle pump to ________________ my back tire.

   c) Aunt Patty used sandpaper to smooth out the ________________ surface.

   d) The mother ________________ used her trunk to cuddle her baby.

   e) Mom cut an apple in ________________ so Dawn and I could share it.

   f) An ________________ is an animal that can live in the water and on land.

   g) The man wiped the ________________ with disinfectant to kill the germs.

   h) Mrs. West got a good ________________ for her big baskets of vegetables.

   i) We found an ________________ kitten crying in the park. I brought it home.

   j) The beef was cooked for hours, but it was still ________________.

Brain Stretch

How many spelling words can you fit into one sentence and still make sense? Give it a try!

Spelling Week 20 – Word Study

A ***metaphor*** is a figure of speech that compares two things that are not alike but have something in common. Metaphors compare by saying something ***is*** something else. Metaphors do **not** use the words ***like*** or ***as*** to compare.

*Example: The stars **are** sparkling diamonds in the night sky.*

1. Write a metaphor to complete the sentence. Remember not to use ***like*** or ***as***.

   a) My toes are ______________________________ when I play in the snow.

   b) The sun is a ______________________________ in the evening sky.

   c) Freshy baked bread is ______________________________ to my nose.

   d) My bedroom is a ______________________________ when I'm feeling sad.

   e) Gently falling snowflakes are ______________________________.

   f) The stormy sea is ______________________________.

   g) Thunder is ______________________________.

2. A ***synonym*** is a word that means the same as another word.

   Circle the synonym for the bolded word.

   a) **rough** dirty scratchy b) **tough** slippery strong

3. An ***antonym*** is a word that has the opposite meaning of another word.

   Circle the antonym for the bolded word.

   a) **laugh** cry angry b) **phony** fake real

Spelling Week 20 – Word Study

1. Use the word list below to look for the words in the puzzle.

   Circle the word in the word search puzzle. Then cross out the word in the list.

S	T	U	F	F	I	N	G	A
A	P	H	I	D	M	N	O	V
K	H	C	O	U	G	H	P	K
M	O	F	A	N	G	S	H	Y
U	N	R	H	Y	P	H	E	N
F	E	O	M	W	T	X	R	G
F	L	U	F	F	Y	D	F	E
L	Y	P	H	O	T	O	I	H
E	N	Y	M	P	H	M	S	J
R	O	U	G	H	Y	U	G	Z

aphid	**cough**	**fangs**	**fluffy**	**gopher**	**hyphen**
muffler	**nymph**	**phone**	**photo**	**rough**	**stuffing**

2. Write a word that rhymes with the word below. The word does not have to be spelled the same.

   a) laugh ________________ b) rough ______________ c) face ________________

   d) feet ________________ e) fudge ______________ f) phone ________________

   g) sphinx ________________ h) finch ______________ i) file ________________

Spelling Week 21 – Consonant Digraphs: *ch, sh, th,* and *wh*

Say each word out loud. Listen for the different sounds the digraphs make.

Copy and spell each word three times using colours of your choice.

1. kitchen __________ __________ __________
2. crusher __________ __________ __________
3. nowhere __________ __________ __________
4. channel __________ __________ __________
5. finish __________ __________ __________
6. archer __________ __________ __________
7. gather __________ __________ __________
8. within __________ __________ __________
9. clothes __________ __________ __________
10. whine __________ __________ __________

Brain Stretch

- Create a word search puzzle based on the spelling words.
- On a piece of paper, write a sentence using each spelling word.

Spelling Week 21 – Consonant Digraphs: *ch, sh, th,* and *wh*

archer	**channel**	**clothes**	**crusher**	**finish**
gather	**kitchen**	**nowhere**	**whine**	**within**

1. Fill in the blank using the best spelling word from the list.

   a) Whenever we go to leave the house, our dog starts to ___________________.

   b) My baby brother found the TV remote and lost my favourite ___________________.

   c) Mom said to bring her all my dirty ___________________ so she can wash them.

   d) Robin Hood was a highly skilled ___________________. He could split an arrow.

   e) To make homemade ice cream, it is best to have an ice ___________________.

   f) I looked everywhere for the matching sock, but it was ___________________.

   g) In the fall, many different types of birds ___________________ at our feeder.

   h) I will ___________________ my homework before I work on my jigsaw puzzle.

   i) My friend Kayla said she would call me back ___________________ 10 minutes.

   j) For Dad's birthday, we work in the ___________________ to make a special meal.

Brain Stretch

How many spelling words can you fit into one sentence and still make sense? Give it a try!

Spelling Week 21 – Word Study

1. Write the correct digraph letters in the word. Use ***ch***, ***sh***, ***th***, or ***wh***.
   Say the word out loud to check.

   a) ben_______ b) _______under c) _______ingles d) fif_______

   e) di_______ f) _______imp g) _______ich h) _______eap

   i) _______ing j) _______isper k) spla_______ l) _______ale

2. How many words can you make? Use only ***ch, sh, th,*** and ***wh*** and the letters given to make the words. Say the word out loud to make sure it's a real word. Write your words on the line.

   Examples: am wham sham

   a) ip ______________________________

   b) ick ______________________________

   c) wi ______________________________

   d) at ______________________________

   e) en ______________________________

   f) in ______________________________

   g) eat ______________________________

   h) ose ______________________________

Spelling Week 21 – Word Study

archer	**channel**	**clothes**	**crusher**	**finish**
gather	**kitchen**	**nowhere**	**whine**	**within**

1. Write the correct spelling word from the list to match the clue.

   a) To bring a task or an activity to an end; to complete ____________________

   b) Something or someone that crushes ____________________

   c) Inside something ____________________

   d) A person who shoots at a target with a bow and arrow ____________________

   e) Items worn to cover the body ____________________

   f) To come or bring together in a group, mass, or unit ____________________

   g) To give or make a long, high-pitched complaining cry ____________________

   h) Not anywhere ____________________

   i) A specific station on a radio or television ____________________

   j) The room in which food is prepared and cooked ____________________

2. Do <u>**not**</u> use the spelling word list for this activity. Write a word that has the given consonant digraphs. These letters can be anywhere in the word.

   a) ch ____________________ b) sh ____________________

   c) th ____________________ d) wh ____________________

Spelling Week 22 – Consonant Blends: ***scr, spl, spr,*** and ***str***

Say each word out loud. Listen to the sounds each consonant blend makes.

Copy and spell each word three times using colours of your choice.

1. splinter __________ __________ __________
2. scratch __________ __________ __________
3. split __________ __________ __________
4. stroller __________ __________ __________
5. scream __________ __________ __________
6. sprig __________ __________ __________
7. sprinkle __________ __________ __________
8. structure __________ __________ __________
9. scrape __________ __________ __________
10. stranger __________ __________ __________

Brain Stretch

- Create a word search puzzle based on the spelling words.
- On a piece of paper, write a sentence using each spelling word.

Spelling Week 22 – Consonant Blends: *scr, spl, spr,* and *str*

scrape	**scratch**	**scream**	**splinter**	**split**
sprig	**sprinkle**	**stranger**	**stroller**	**structure**

1. Fill in the blank using the best spelling word from the list.

   a) My sister let out a loud ________________ when she saw the big spider.

   b) Jerry forgot his lunch, so I offered to ________________ my lunch with him.

   c) Sally is always strapped into her ________________ when she goes for walks.

   d) Grandma said we could ________________ tiny candies on top of our ice cream.

   e) Mom will ________________ the hot sweet potato out of its skin to make pie.

   f) After chasing the cat, our dog Buster had a big ________________ on his nose.

   g) Sam built a tall ________________ out of wooden craft sticks glued together.

   h) Milly got a big wood ________________ in her finger from the deck railing.

   i) Dad puts a small ________________ of green parsley on top of the fish.

   j) There's a ________________ sitting by the library, playing a guitar and singing.

Brain Stretch

How many spelling words can you fit into one sentence and still make sense? Give it a try!

Spelling Week 22 – Word Study

Write a short story using as many of these new words as you can.

scrape	**scratch**	**scream**	**splinter**	**split**
sprig	**sprinkle**	**stranger**	**stroller**	**structure**

Spelling Week 22 – Word Study

1. Use the word list below to look for the words in the puzzle.

   Circle the word in the puzzle. Then cross out the word in the list.

S	P	L	A	T	T	E	R	S
C	W	S	P	R	I	N	G	P
R	S	P	L	O	T	C	H	R
A	P	L	S	T	R	U	T	A
M	R	A	S	U	S	S	O	I
B	U	S	T	R	I	N	G	N
L	C	H	T	F	G	D	F	E
E	E	S	C	R	U	F	F	Y
I	S	T	R	I	K	E	B	J
S	C	R	E	E	N	H	G	Z

scramble	**screen**	**scruffy**	**splash**	**splatter**	**splotch**
sprain	**spring**	**spruce**	**strike**	**string**	**strut**

2. Write ***scr, spl, spr,*** or ***str*** to make a word. Make sure to say the word out loud to check it.

a) _______unch　　b) _______eet　　c) _______itz

d) _______eam　　e) _______ub　　f) _______at

g) _______ipt　　h) _______ayer　　i) _______ength

j) _______out　　k) _______ipes　　l) _______ead

Spelling Week 23 – *R*-controlled Vowels with ***or, er, ir, ur,*** and ***ear***

When the letter ***r*** follows a vowel, it changes the sound of the vowel.

Examples: *cat car* *box born* *gift girl* *vet verb* *cut curl*

Say each word out loud. Listen to how the vowels are pronounced. Copy and spell each word three times using colours of your choice.

1. person ________ ________ ________
2. turkey ________ ________ ________
3. force ________ ________ ________
4. thirty ________ ________ ________
5. during ________ ________ ________
6. squirm ________ ________ ________
7. heard ________ ________ ________
8. nervous ________ ________ ________
9. sports ________ ________ ________
10. early ________ ________ ________

Spelling Week 23 – *R*-controlled Vowels with ***or, er, ir, ur,*** and ***ear***

during	**early**	**force**	**heard**	**nervous**
person	**sports**	**squirm**	**thirty**	**turkey**

1. Fill in the blank using the best spelling word from the list.

   a) Dad made ____________________ cupcakes for our class bake sale.

   b) Soccer and baseball are my favourite ____________________.

   c) My stomach started to growl very loudly ____________________ the movie.

   d) The door was stuck shut, so my father had to ____________________ it open.

   e) We went outside ____________________ in the morning to catch the meteor shower.

   f) Tammy ____________________ a strange bird singing this morning.

   g) Robert gets very ____________________ when he has to give reports to the class.

   h) Mrs. Williams is a sculptor and a painter. He is a very busy ____________________.

   i) The tiny caterpillar began to ____________________ when I picked it up.

   j) A large male wild ____________________ is standing on our front awn.

Brain Stretch

How many spelling words can you fit into one sentence and still make sense? Give it a try!

Spelling Week 23 – Word Study

The letter combinations listed below all make an ***er*** sound, however, that's not always true. The same letter combination can make different sounds. For example, in the word ***work***, the ***or*** as an ***er*** sound, but in the word ***pork*** it does not. Also, when a vowel is followed by a **consonant + *e, i,* or *y***, the vowel usually says its name (***a, e, i, o,*** or ***u***). When that happens, the same combination of letters don't have an ***er*** sound, such as in the words ***her*** and ***here***.

1. Write a word with an ***er*** sound made by the given letters. Then write a word with the same letter combination that does not make an ***er*** sound.

   Examples: first hire pearl gear fur pour were here tern steer work pork

   a) ir ______________________________

   b) er ______________________________

   c) ur ______________________________

   d) or ______________________________

   e) ear ______________________________

2. ***Homophones*** are words that sound the same, but are spelled differently. Read the word. Write its homophone on the line.

   Examples: reed read red read blew blue

   a) route ____________ b) creak ____________ c) due ____________

   d) mooed ____________ e) pale ____________ f) not ____________

   g) higher ____________ h) wood ____________ i) hear ____________

   j) dear ____________ k) pause ____________ l) plain ____________

Spelling Week 23 – Word Study

during	**early**	**force**	**heard**	**nervous**
person	**sports**	**squirm**	**thirty**	**turkey**

1. Write the correct spelling word from the list to match the clue.

a) A human being regarded as an individual ____________________

b) Throughout the course or duration of a period of time ____________________

c) Strength or energy as an attribute of physical action or movement; to break open or push hard; any interaction that will change the motion of an object ____________________

d) Happening or done before the usual or expected time ____________________

e) To wriggle or twist the body from side to side from nervousness or discomfort ____________________

f) Worried and anxious ____________________

g) Perceived with the ear the sound made by someone or something ____________________

h) The number word halfway between twenty and forty ____________________

i) A large bird with a bald head and a wattle, that is often used for food on special occasions such as Thanksgiving and Christmas ____________________

j) Activities involving physical exertion and skill from a team or an individual competing with another person or team ____________________

Spelling Week 24 – *R*-controlled Vowels with ***ar, are, or,*** and ***ore***

The letter ***r*** changes the way vowels sound, such as in the words ***fog*** and ***fort***.

The letters ***or*** and ***ore*** usually make the same sound.

Examples: *torn* *tore* *fork* *forest*

The letters ***ar*** and ***are*** usually sound different.

Examples: *car* *care* *star* *stare*

Say each word out loud. Listen to the sound of the vowels before the ***r***.

Copy and spell each word three times using colours of your choice.

1. shore ______ ______ ______
2. parents ______ ______ ______
3. factory ______ ______ ______
4. care ______ ______ ______
5. parcel ______ ______ ______
6. farmer ______ ______ ______
7. chores ______ ______ ______
8. normal ______ ______ ______
9. monitor ______ ______ ______
10. gorilla ______ ______ ______

Spelling Week 24 – *R*-controlled Vowels with ***ar, are, or,*** and ***ore***

care	**cart**	**chores**	**factory**	**farmer**
gorilla	**monitor**	**parcel**	**parents**	**shore**

1. Fill in the blank using the best spelling word from the list.

   a) Our cats Max and Patty are very good ________________ to their five kittens.

   b) We collect shells whenever we walk along the ________________ at the beach.

   c) I'm learning to ________________ for our new puppy.

   d) The ________________ up the road allows people to pick strawberries in June.

   e) Terry is allowed to come out to play after he finishes his ________________.

   f) My mother is waiting for a ________________ to arrive from the post office.

   g) Franny is afraid of the big ________________ at the zoo.

   h) My grandparents sell vegetables from a ________________ at their farm.

   i) The toys in the store are made in a big ________________ in Toronto.

   j) Mom and Dad listen to my baby sister on the ________________ in her room.

Brain Stretch

How many spelling words can you fit into one sentence and still make sense? Give it a try!

Spelling Week 24 – Word Study

1. On the lines below, write these words in alphabetical order.

fork **mark** **import** **born** **part** **hare**

a) ____________ b) ____________ c) ____________

d) ____________ e) ____________ f) ____________

2. Write a short sentence using the word below. Check your punctation.

a) spark ____________

b) core ____________

c) mark ____________

d) fork ____________

e) scare ____________

f) storm ____________

g) bark ____________

h) tore ____________

i) dare ____________

Spelling Week 24 – Word Study

1. Use the word list below to look for the words in the puzzle.

   Circle the word in the word search puzzle. Then cross out the word in the list.

F	A	R	M	E	R	A	S	B
L	S	O	R	T	E	D	M	O
A	R	P	E	C	O	O	A	R
R	I	S	N	O	R	E	R	D
E	G	C	E	U	S	S	T	E
A	N	A	R	S	E	E	R	R
H	O	R	S	E	P	D	W	E
W	R	Y	P	Y	I	A	O	H
I	E	U	A	I	K	M	R	J
B	A	R	K	I	N	G	E	K

barking **border** **farmer** **flare** **horse** **ignore**

park **scary** **smart** **snore** **sorted** **wore**

2. Write a word that rhymes with the word below. The word does not have to be spelled the same.

   a) score ________________ b) park ________________ c) torn________________

   d) mare ________________ e) sport ________________ f) tarp ________________

   g) cord ________________ h) caret ________________ i) spork ________________

Spelling Week 25 – Homophones and Homographs

Say each word out loud. Listen for the words that sound the same.

Copy and spell each word three times using colours of your choice.

1. piece ______ ______ ______
2. knight ______ ______ ______
3. write ______ ______ ______
4. reed ______ ______ ______
5. night ______ ______ ______
6. knew ______ ______ ______
7. peace ______ ______ ______
8. right ______ ______ ______
9. new ______ ______ ______
10. read ______ ______ ______

Brain Stretch

- Create a word search puzzle based on the spelling words.
- On a piece of paper, write a sentence using each spelling word.

Spelling Week 25 – Homophones and Homographs

knew	**knight**	**new**	**night**	**peace**
piece	**read**	**reed**	**right**	**write**

1. Fill in the blank using the best spelling word from the list.

   a) In fairytales, the good ____________________ always defeats the evil dragon.

   b) I love the ____________________ and quiet of mornings at the cottage.

   c) I'm studying because I want to make sure I get the answers ____________________.

   d) Aunt Alice gave me a small ____________________ of pumpkin pie.

   e) For literacy class, we have to ____________________ six Aesop's fables.

   f) Ted was the silliest dog I ever ____________________.

   g) Gail got some brand ____________________ shoes for going back to school.

   h) The other ____________________, we saw a bunch of shooting stars in the sky.

   i) A red-winged blackbird was perched on a tall ____________________ in the pond.

   j) Mr. Smith said to ____________________ the poem in our notebooks.

Brain Stretch

How many spelling words can you fit into one sentence and still make sense? Give it a try!

Spelling Week 25 – Word Study

1. Draw a line from the word in the left column to its homophone in the right column.

a) ant	fined
b) banned	bored
c) stare	maid
d) find	band
e) hire	stair
f) board	aunt
g) made	higher

2. Circle the word that goes with the definition.

a) **hair** **hare** type of large rabbit with long ears

b) **stare** **stair** look at someone or something for a long time

c) **pale** **pail** very light in colour

d) **sale** **sail** part of a ship that catches the wind to help the ship move

e) **real** **reel** cylinder on which film, thread, or wire can be wound

f) **reed** **read** tall, grass plant that grows in water or marshes

g) **heel** **heal** become healthy again

Spelling Week 25 – Word Study

1. Use the word list below to look for the words in the puzzle.

Circle the word in the word search puzzle. Then cross out the word in the list.

P	A	D	D	E	D	A	X	M
A	K	I	D	L	M	N	R	I
T	N	M	I	S	T	O	A	S
T	O	J	C	F	I	I	Y	S
E	W	R	O	U	T	E	S	E
D	S	O	W	P	H	Q	R	D
V	H	E	R	D	G	D	O	E
R	A	I	S	E	I	L	O	H
I	S	L	N	O	S	E	T	J
H	E	A	R	D	Y	U	W	Z

heard **herd** **knows** **missed** **mist** **nose**

padded **patted** **raise** **rays** **root** **route**

2. Draw a line to the meaning of the homograph below.

a) bow [boh] dived down

b) bow [bow] bend down gracefully to show respect

c) dove [duhv] type of bird similar to a pigeon

d) dove [dohv] sharp-tipped object that is shot with an arrow

Spelling Week 1 – Test

Name: ______________________

Listen to the spelling words. Print each spelling word.

1. ______________________
2. ______________________
3. ______________________
4. ______________________
5. ______________________
6. ______________________
7. ______________________
8. ______________________
9. ______________________
10. ______________________

Bonus

1. ______________________
2. ______________________

Spelling Week 2 – Test

Name: ______________________

Listen to the spelling words. Print each spelling word.

1. ______________________
2. ______________________
3. ______________________
4. ______________________
5. ______________________
6. ______________________
7. ______________________
8. ______________________
9. ______________________
10. ______________________

Bonus

1. ______________________
2. ______________________

Spelling Week 3 – Test

Name: ______________________

Listen to the spelling words. Print each spelling word.

1. ____________ 6. ____________

2. ____________ 7. ____________

3. ____________ 8. ____________

4. ____________ 9. ____________

5. ____________ 10. ____________

Bonus

1. ____________ 2. ____________

Spelling Week 4 – Test

Name: ______________________

Listen to the spelling words. Print each spelling word.

1. ____________ 6. ____________

2. ____________ 7. ____________

3. ____________ 8. ____________

4. ____________ 9. ____________

5. ____________ 10. ____________

Bonus

1. ____________ 2. ____________

Spelling Week 5 – Test

Name: ______________________________

Listen to the spelling words. Print each spelling word.

1. ______________________________
2. ______________________________
3. ______________________________
4. ______________________________
5. ______________________________
6. ______________________________
7. ______________________________
8. ______________________________
9. ______________________________
10. ______________________________

Bonus

1. ______________________________
2. ______________________________

Spelling Week 6 – Test

Name: ______________________________

Listen to the spelling words. Print each spelling word.

1. ______________________________
2. ______________________________
3. ______________________________
4. ______________________________
5. ______________________________
6. ______________________________
7. ______________________________
8. ______________________________
9. ______________________________
10. ______________________________

Bonus

1. ______________________________
2. ______________________________

Spelling Week 7 – Test

Name: ____________________

Listen to the spelling words. Print each spelling word.

1. ____________________
2. ____________________
3. ____________________
4. ____________________
5. ____________________
6. ____________________
7. ____________________
8. ____________________
9. ____________________
10. ____________________

Bonus

1. ____________________
2. ____________________

Spelling Week 8 – Test

Name: ____________________

Listen to the spelling words. Print each spelling word.

1. ____________________
2. ____________________
3. ____________________
4. ____________________
5. ____________________
6. ____________________
7. ____________________
8. ____________________
9. ____________________
10. ____________________

Bonus

1. ____________________
2. ____________________

Spelling Week 9 – Test

Name: ______________________

Listen to the spelling words. Print each spelling word.

1. ______________________
2. ______________________
3. ______________________
4. ______________________
5. ______________________
6. ______________________
7. ______________________
8. ______________________
9. ______________________
10. ______________________

Bonus

1. ______________________
2. ______________________

Spelling Week 10 – Test

Name: ______________________

Listen to the spelling words. Print each spelling word.

1. ______________________
2. ______________________
3. ______________________
4. ______________________
5. ______________________
6. ______________________
7. ______________________
8. ______________________
9. ______________________
10. ______________________

Bonus

1. ______________________
2. ______________________

Spelling Week 11 – Test

Name: ______________________

Listen to the spelling words. Print each spelling word.

1. ____________ 6. ____________

2. ____________ 7. ____________

3. ____________ 8. ____________

4. ____________ 9. ____________

5. ____________ 10. ____________

Bonus

1. ____________ 2. ____________

Spelling Week 12 – Test

Name: ______________________

Listen to the spelling words. Print each spelling word.

1. ____________ 6. ____________

2. ____________ 7. ____________

3. ____________ 8. ____________

4. ____________ 9. ____________

5. ____________ 10. ____________

Bonus

1. ____________ 2. ____________

Spelling Week 13 – Test

Name: ______________________

Listen to the spelling words. Print each spelling word.

1. ______________________
2. ______________________
3. ______________________
4. ______________________
5. ______________________
6. ______________________
7. ______________________
8. ______________________
9. ______________________
10. ______________________

Bonus

1. ______________________
2. ______________________

Spelling Week 14 – Test

Name: ______________________

Listen to the spelling words. Print each spelling word.

1. ______________________
2. ______________________
3. ______________________
4. ______________________
5. ______________________
6. ______________________
7. ______________________
8. ______________________
9. ______________________
10. ______________________

Bonus

1. ______________________
2. ______________________

Spelling Week 15 – Test

Name: ______________________

Listen to the spelling words. Print each spelling word.

1. ______________________
2. ______________________
3. ______________________
4. ______________________
5. ______________________
6. ______________________
7. ______________________
8. ______________________
9. ______________________
10. ______________________

Bonus

1. ______________________
2. ______________________

Spelling Week 16 – Test

Name: ______________________

Listen to the spelling words. Print each spelling word.

1. ______________________
2. ______________________
3. ______________________
4. ______________________
5. ______________________
6. ______________________
7. ______________________
8. ______________________
9. ______________________
10. ______________________

Bonus

1. ______________________
2. ______________________

Spelling Week 17 – Test

Name: ____________________

Listen to the spelling words. Print each spelling word.

1. ____________________
2. ____________________
3. ____________________
4. ____________________
5. ____________________
6. ____________________
7. ____________________
8. ____________________
9. ____________________
10. ____________________

Bonus

1. ____________________
2. ____________________

Spelling Week 18 – Test

Name: ____________________

Listen to the spelling words. Print each spelling word.

1. ____________________
2. ____________________
3. ____________________
4. ____________________
5. ____________________
6. ____________________
7. ____________________
8. ____________________
9. ____________________
10. ____________________

Bonus

1. ____________________
2. ____________________

Spelling Week 19 – Test

Name: ____________________

Listen to the spelling words. Print each spelling word.

1. ____________________
2. ____________________
3. ____________________
4. ____________________
5. ____________________
6. ____________________
7. ____________________
8. ____________________
9. ____________________
10. ____________________

Bonus

1. ____________________
2. ____________________

Spelling Week 20 – Test

Name: ____________________

Listen to the spelling words. Print each spelling word.

1. ____________________
2. ____________________
3. ____________________
4. ____________________
5. ____________________
6. ____________________
7. ____________________
8. ____________________
9. ____________________
10. ____________________

Bonus

1. ____________________
2. ____________________

Spelling Week 21 – Test

Name: ______________________

Listen to the spelling words. Print each spelling word.

1. ______________ 6. ______________
2. ______________ 7. ______________
3. ______________ 8. ______________
4. ______________ 9. ______________
5. ______________ 10. ______________

Bonus

1. ______________ 2. ______________

Spelling Week 22 – Test

Name: ______________________

Listen to the spelling words. Print each spelling word.

1. ______________ 7. ______________
2. ______________ 8. ______________
3. ______________ 9. ______________
4. ______________ 10. ______________
5. ______________ 11. ______________
6. ______________ 12. ______________

Spelling Week 23 – Test

Name: ______________________

Listen to the spelling words. Print each spelling word.

1. ______________ 6. ______________

2. ______________ 7. ______________

3. ______________ 8. ______________

4. ______________ 9. ______________

5. ______________ 10. ______________

Bonus

1. ______________ 2. ______________

Spelling Week 24 – Test

Name: ______________________

Listen to the spelling words. Print each spelling word.

1. ______________ 6. ______________

2. ______________ 7. ______________

3. ______________ 8. ______________

4. ______________ 9. ______________

5. ______________ 10. ______________

Bonus

1. ______________ 2. ______________

Spelling Week 25 – Test

Name: ______________________________

Listen to the spelling words. Print each spelling word.

1. ____________________
2. ____________________
3. ____________________
4. ____________________
5. ____________________
6. ____________________
7. ____________________
8. ____________________
9. ____________________
10. ____________________

Bonus

1. ____________________
2. ____________________

Answers

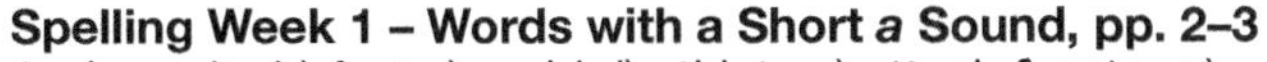

Spelling Week 1 – Words with a Short *a* Sound, pp. 2–3
1. a) gravity b) fact c) rapid d) athlete e) attach f) actor g) clasp h) glance i) canvas j) adventure

Spelling Week 1 – Word Study, p. 4
1. a) scrap b) tap c) lack d) sham e) They all end in an e.
2. a) attach b) fact c) rapid d) gravity e) canvas f) athlete g) actor h) glance i) clasp
3. a) glance: to take a brief look b) attach: to join things together c) adventure: an unusual and exciting activity or experience d) rapid: very quick or fast e) fact: something that is known to be true f) clasp: an interlocking device used to fasten things together

Spelling Week 1 – Word Study, p. 5
1.

R	A	B	B	I	T	C	O	J
G	C	A	M	C	O	V	A	L
B	A	N	A	N	A	V	H	A
A	N	T	T	C	H	J	A	S
S	V	R	C	U	S	C	P	T
A	A	J	H	Q	X	E	P	T
T	S	D	A	N	C	E	Y	P
I	Y	I	L	F	A	X	P	A
N	S	D	A	C	T	O	R	C
A	F	L	A	S	H	U	Z	K

2. a) slap, laugh flappy b) blanket, taller, sandwich c) wrapper, package, taffy, crabby

Spelling Week 2 – Words with a Short *e* Sound, pp. 6–7
1. a) metal b) address c) peculiar d) entrance e) permit f) ancestor g) arrest h) kept i) distress
j) venture

Spelling Week 2 – Word Study, p. 8
1. a) kettle, spell, letters, felt b) leopard, teller, feather, shell c) breakfast, lemon, health d) barrel, tent, elephant e) dent, slept, rest
2. a) went b) pet c) carpet d) present
3. Sample answers: If I turn left at the end of my street, I can see the library. I accidentally left my favourite hat at school.

Spelling Week 2 – Word Study, p. 9
1. a) metal b) entrance c) peculiar d) venture e) ancestor f) address g) arrest h) permit i) kept
2. Sample answers: a) mess, dress, caress, tress, confess b) smell, shell, well, spell, fell, tell
c) melt, welt d) wrench, bench, stench e) lend, end, send, fend, vend, bend f) better, setter,
getter

Spelling Week 3 – Words with a Short *i* Sound, pp. 10–11
1. a) apricot b) bandit c) mixture d) garlic e) English f) dimple g) centimetre h) deposit i) chicken
j) alligator

Spelling Week 3 – Word Study, p. 12
1. a) whistle b) King c) squished
2. a) its b) knit c) which d) build e) inn f) lynx
3. a) 2 syllables b) 5 syllables c) 1 syllable

4. Sample answers: The black pants fit me perfectly. My family exercises and eats well so we can all keep fit.

Spelling Week 3 – Word Study, p. 12

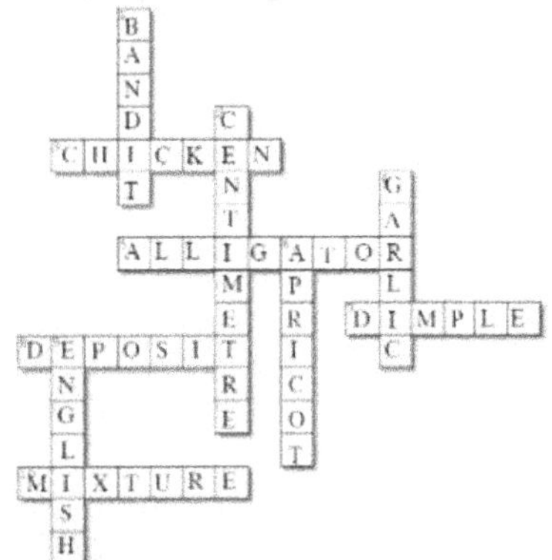

Spelling Week 4 – Words with a Short *o* Sound, pp. 14–15
1. a) oxen b) copper c) dolphin d) rhombus e) bother f) fossil g) lodge h) across i) monster j) solve

Spelling Week 4 – Word Study, p. 16
1. a) copper b) oxen c) monster d) solve
2. Sample answers: a) rot, fought, clot, lot, spot, shot, cot, caught b) rock, talk, mock, sock, squawk c) father d) socks, talks, mocks, squawks e) stop, shop, top, mop, lop f) off, scoff, trough g) tot, lot, spot, shot, bot h) moss, boss, toss i) fox, talks, socks, rocks, squawks
3. a) bossy, tonic, softly b) tropical, glob, blond c) pocket, long, hospital

Spelling Week 4 – Word Study, p. 17
1. a) oxen b) solve c) copper d) lodge e) monster f) rhombus g) fossil h) bother i) across j) dolphin
2. a) dolphin b) across c) copper d) fossil e) bother f) rhombus

Spelling Week 5 – Words with a Short *u* Sound, pp. 18–19
1. a) nugget b) subject c) pumpkin d) crumble e) knuckle f) jungle g) muffin h) husband
i) umbrella j) vulture

Spelling Week 5 – Word Study, p. 20
1. a) aloud, though b) pounce, cough c) spout, cute d) crouch, through, guess
2. a) circle b and fl; cross out v b) circle gl and m; cross out k c) circle c and gr; cross out d
d) circle bl and th; cross out p e) circle fl and p; cross out br f) circle c and th; cross out m

Spelling Week 5 – Word Study, p. 21

1.

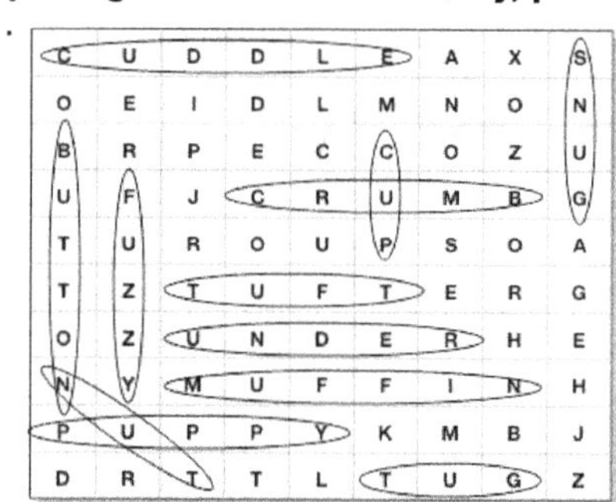

2. Sample answers: a) lunch, crunch, hunch b) tough, cuff, scuff, muff c) yummy, mummy, dummy d) humble, bumble, tumble, stumble e) thunder, wonder, under f) grumpy, stumpy, dumpy, bumpy

Spelling Week 6 – Words with a Long *a* Sound, pp. 22–23

1. a) decade b) generate c) display d) able e) elevator f) frame g) chain h) nail i) became j) scale

Spelling Week 6 – Word Study, p. 24

1. a) stair, take, whale b) shape, lazy, crate c) taste, grain d) grade, make, away e) space, hair, aim
2. A, J, K
3. 8, 18, 28, 38, 48, 58, 68, 78, 80, 81, 82, 83, 84, 85, 86, 87, 88, 89, 98

Spelling Week 6 – Word Study, p. 25

1.

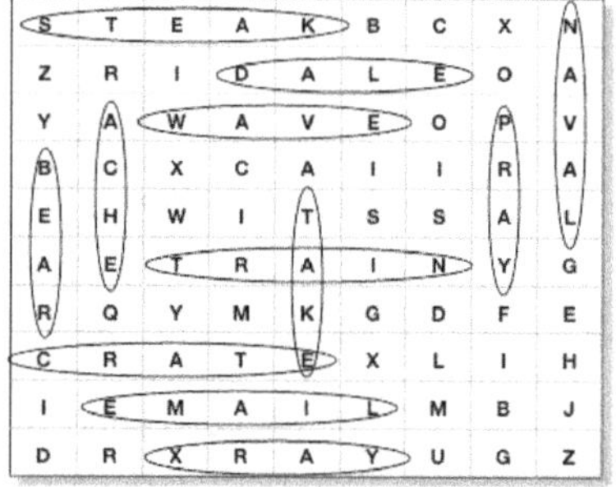

2. Sample answers: a) care, bear, rare, air, stare, stair, dare, pear, pair b) take, sake, fake, make, ache, shake, rake c) came, tame, lame, fame, shame d) taste, waist, waste, paced, raced, aced e) day, say, ray, lay, way, hay, stay, pay, delay f) gain, main, lane, rain, sane, cane, again, train, plane, plain, strain, crane

Spelling Week 7 – Words with a Long *e* Sound, pp. 26–27

1. a) fifteen b) really c) kilometre d) release e) complete f) breeze g) become h) relief i) secret j) delete

Spelling Week 7 – Word Study, p. 28

1. a) become b) complete c) relief d) secret e) breeze f) fifteen g) really h) kilometre i) delete
2. e, ee, ea, ie, y, ey, and an e followed by a consonant + e
3. Ontario and British Columbia
4. a) hand/made, under/wear, sail/boat b) sea/star, dog/house, back/yard c) home/work, finger/nail, row/boat d) eye/lash, head/ache, sky/line

Spelling Week 7 – Word Study, p. 29

1. a) kilometre b) delete c) really d) become e) release f) complete g) fifteen h) breeze i) secret j) relief
2. Sample answers: a) feed, speech, seek, leek, keen, seen, been, free, greet, greedy b) field, believe, belief, brief, chief, niece, priest, siege, achieve, piece c) funny, bunny, runny, sunny, monkey, donkey, galley, alley, valley d) weak, dear, fear, gear, leaf, steal, meal, real, deal, heal, seal, zeal, appeal, squeal, read

Spelling Week 8 – Words with a Long *i* Sound, pp. 30–31

1. a) ninety b) choir c) describe d) fragile e) crocodile f) awhile g) decide h) inside i) violin j) beside

Spelling Week 8 – Word Study, p. 32

1. a) shine, sigh, sky b) slight, while, cry c) tile, sign, rhyme, bike d) grime, fight, lining e) spice, dried, hire
2. a) okay b) sneaky
3. a) yours b) lose
4. five, nine
5. Sample answers: live, drive, dive, survive, arrive; mine, line, spine, fine, dine, wine, whine, shine

Spelling Week 8 – Word Study, p. 33

1.

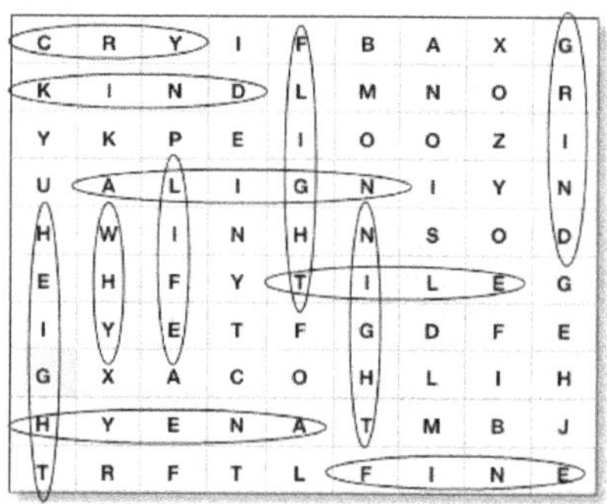

2. Sample answers: a) line, spine, mine, wine, shine b) like, trike, spike c) lie, die, cry, sigh, dry, fry, spy, shy d) while, file, mile, bile e) cry, dry, fry f) wide, glide, cried, fried, dried

Spelling Week 9 – Words with a Long *o* Sound, pp. 34–35

1. a) solo b) trio c) pueblo d) moment e) Although f) poet g) rodeo h) vocal i) lower j) window

Spelling Week 9 – Word Study, p. 36

1. Marco and his family took a trip to the zoo. Most of them were excited to see all the animals. But his cousin Lori didn't want to go. She was afraid of the hippos and polar bears. Her cousins Tony and Marco held her hand and told her about each animal as they went. There was so much to learn! When she saw the hippos rolling in the water, she started to laugh. The hippos were having fun! The polar bears were playing with a ball. They were having fun, too! One old bear was sleeping. Lori and her family were safe

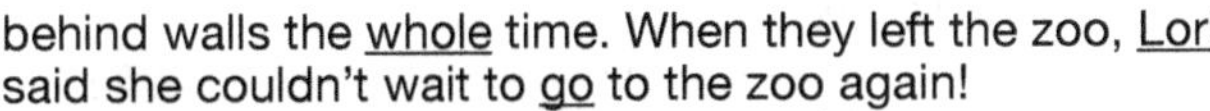

behind walls the whole time. When they left the zoo, Lori said she couldn't wait to go to the zoo again!
2. a) trio b) rodeo c) vocal d) window e) lower
3. a) group b) shrink
4. developing and increasing in ability

Spelling Week 9 – Word Study, p. 37
1. a) lower b) pueblo c) rodeo d) poet e) solo f) window g) vocal h) trio i) although j) moment
2. Sample answers: a) toe, foe, hoe, doe, oboe b) float, boat, coat, goat, moat, stoat, oat, groan, toast, goal, loaf, load, road, roam c) grow, glow, flow, know, show, slow, snow, growth, narrow, sparrow, furrow, barrow, tomorrow d) go, no, so, banjo, bonus, focus, comb, total, piano, solo, trio (Note: Words with a consonant + e are also acceptable. Sample answers: bone, tone, phone, alone, stroke, stole, store, etc.

Spelling Week 10 – Words with a Long *u* Sound, pp. 38–39
1. a) askew b) jewel c) pupil d) university e) utensil f) commute g) amuse h) computer i) bugle
j) acute

Spelling Week 10 – Word Study, p. 40
1. a) rescue, cute, unit b) university, menu, yule c) music, argue, cue d) few, view, unite
2. Sample answers: The human eye has a black pupil. My teacher says I am a very good pupil.
3. Sample answers: Every human being is unique. My best friend wears some very unique clothing. Katy has a very unique hairstyle.

Spelling Week 10 – Word Study, p. 41
1.

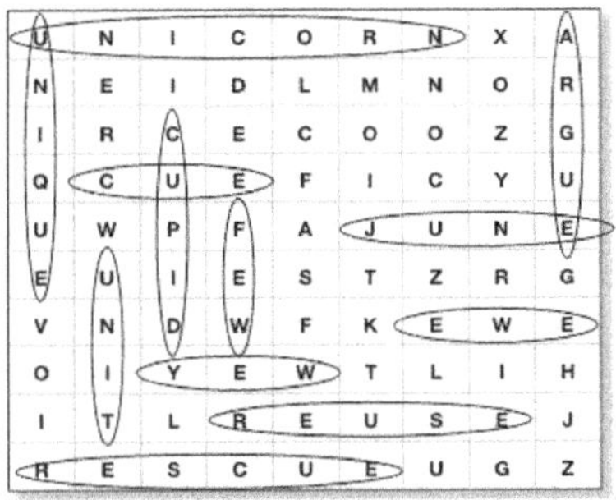

Spelling Week 11 – Words with *y* as Long *i* and Long *e* Sounds, pp. 42–43
1. a) comedy b) dirty c) reply d) monkey e) bytes f) merely g) recycle h) type i) parsley j) anyone

Spelling Week 11 – Word Study, p. 44
1. a) comedy b) anyone c) parsley d) monkey e) recycle f) dirty
2. a) eye + ball, day + dream b) any + one, body + guard c) blue + berry, fire + fly

Spelling Week 11 – Word Study, p. 45
1. a) recycle b_ bytes c) monkey d) dirty e) comedy f) merely g) type h) parsley i) anyone j) reply
2. Sample answers: I will type my story on my laptop. A rose is a type of scented flower.

Spelling Week 12 – Contractions, pp. 46–47
1. a) they're b) can't c) We're d) isn't e) he's f) you'll g) she's h) haven't i) wouldn't j) Isn't

Spelling Week 12 – Word Study, p. 48
1. a) circle "willn't"; won't b) circle "cann't"; can't c) circle "willn't"; won't d) circle "cant"; can't
e) circle "Donot"; Don't f) circle "Hasnot"; Hasn't
2. a) could not b) had not c) we have d) she is e) that is f) cannot g) is not h) will not i) you are j) did not

Spelling Week 12 – Word Study, p. 49
1. a) It's not what you look at that matters, but what you see. b) Isn't it amazing how a person who was once a stranger can suddenly become your best friend?

Spelling Week 13 – Double Consonants, pp. 50–51
1. a) luggage b) actress c) tossed d) barrel e) puzzle f) afford g) drill h) coton i) hammer
j) occasion

Spelling Week 13 – Word Study, p. 52
1. a) spelled; spelling b) knitted; knitting c) folded; folding d) planned; planning e) walked; walking
2. a) **X**; folding b) ✔ c) ✔ d) **X**; mashing e) ✔ f) **X**; melting g) ✔ h) **X**; talking

Spelling Week 13 – Word Study, p. 53
1.

S	N	U	G	G	L	E	T	M
D	O	L	L	A	R	M	U	U
C	U	P	P	E	R	A	G	F
U	S	H	O	P	Z	T	G	F
D	B	T	H	W	O	T	E	I
D	U	F	Y	S	T	E	D	N
L	B	U	K	N	P	R	F	E
E	B	Z	B	U	Z	Z	E	R
I	L	Z	T	A	L	L	E	R
D	E	Y	P	U	P	P	Y	Z

2. Sample answers: a) pill, bill, spill, gill, chill, fill, mill, will, grill b) better, petter, getter, letter
c) spiller, filler, chiller, griller d) fatter, patter, spatter, splatter, shatter, clatter e) toss, boss, floss f) any, many g) runny, bunny, sunny, money, honey h) jell, spell, tell, fell, shell, well i) fall, ball, all, mall, call, tall, shawl, wall, crawl

Spelling Week 14 – Words with Silent Letters, pp. 54–55
1. a) chords b) orange c) palm d) whisper e) listening f) calf g) guest h) wrench i) castle j) weigh

Answers

Spelling Week 14 – Word Study, p. 56

1. a) bright, cube, honest b) wheel, unique, yule c) school, argue, walk d) blue, night, listen e) half, crumb, gnome
2. a) care b) spine c) kite d) cute e) note f) scrape g) made h) dime
3. Sample answer: When I add an ***e***, the vowel changes from a short sound to a long sound.
4. one, five, nine
5. Sample answers: one: fun, run, sun, bun, ton, son; five: live, dive, alive, drive, arrive, thrive; nine: fine, mine, line, wine, sign, swine, spine

Spelling Week 14 – Word Study, p. 57

1. a) palm b) listening c) chords d) calf e) whisper f) castle g) guest h) wrench i) weigh j) orange
2. Sample answers: a) write, wrong, wriggle, wrap, wrist, wrinkle, wreck, wreath, wren, wrestle b) ghost, though, although, eight, weight, height, high, thigh, knight, nei c) comb, bomb, tomb, climb, limb d) glisten, hustle, wrestle, bristle, bustle, nestle, rustle, thistle, whistle, trestle

Spelling Week 15 – Words with Long and Short *oo* Sounds, pp. 58–59

1. a) crooked b) bamboo c) loom d) book e) grew f) aloof g) mistook h) stood i) tomb j) would

Spelling Week 15 – Word Study, p. 60

1. a) tuna, blew, true b) glue, crew, fruit c) pool, loose, due d) review, soup, loom
2. a) stood, could, look b) soot, should, woof c) hood, wood, pull d) cookie, brook, foot
3. a) S b) N c) L d) L e) N f) S g) N h) S i) L

Spelling Week 15 – Word Study, p. 61

1.

C	O	O	K	I	E	F	N	A
S	H	O	O	K	M	L	C	V
P	U	L	L	C	S	U	O	X
O	K	H	C	F	I	T	U	B
O	M	O	O	D	V	E	L	L
L	H	O	Y	S	T	E	D	O
V	Q	D	T	F	G	D	F	O
O	Y	A	C	R	E	W	I	M
S	U	I	T	I	K	M	B	J
D	R	F	W	O	U	L	D	Z

2. Sample answers: a) boot, route, suit, scoot b) brook, took, look, hook, nook c) moon, soon, June, rune, croon, balloon, dune, goon, baboon d) room, bloom, plume, tomb, womb e) pull, wool, bull, awful f) blue, blew, knew, new, due, sue, flu, flew, flue, true g) pool, tool, cool h) could, good, would, should, stood, understood

Spelling Week 16 – Words with *oi* and *oy*, pp. 62–63

1. a) poison b) oyster c) choice d) destroy e) voyage f) loyal g) moisture h) avoid i) decoy j) joined

Spelling Week 16 – Word Study, p. 64

1. a) avoid b) oysters c) loyal d) joined e) poison f) voyage
2. a) straw + berry, bath + tub b) camp + fire, cheese + cake c) dough + nut, play + ground

Spelling Week 16 – Word Study, p. 65

1. a) poison b) oyster c) decoy d) joined e) avoid f) voyage g) choice h) destroy i) loyal j) moisture
2. Sample answers: a) joint, point, coin, android, toilet, boil, coil, spoil, soil, toil, voice, oink, noise, noisy b) joy, royal, toy, enjoy, soy, coy, boy, cowboy, gargoyle, ahoy, annoy, alloy, employ

Spelling Week 17 – Words with *ow* and *ou*, pp. 66–67

1. a) brown b) crowd c) count d) pounce e) mountain f) towel g) frown h) browswer i) council j) couch

Spelling Week 17 – Word Study, p. 68

1. a) underline: proud, allow; circle: grow, though, know b) underline: sprout, loud, ground; circle: below, marshmallow c) underline: grouch, fowl; circle: narrow, snow, shadow d) underline: bounce, cloud, scout; circle: throw, pillow
2. a) read: to see and take in the meaning of letters and symbols b) reed: a tall, thin grass-like aquatic plant c) to fly or rise high in the air d) sore: painful and aching e) tail: the end part of an animal f) tale: a story g) thrown: propelled something through the air with force h) the official chair a king or queen sits on

Spelling Week 17 – Word Study, p. 69

1.

F	O	U	N	T	A	I	N	S
E	B	I	G	R	O	U	C	H
L	O	W	E	R	O	O	Z	A
L	R	J	S	F	I	I	Y	L
O	R	C	N	Q	A	T	S	L
W	O	M	O	U	T	H	C	O
V	W	Y	W	F	G	F	O	W
O	Y	A	C	O	L	L	U	H
P	O	U	T	I	O	M	R	J
N	A	R	R	O	W	U	G	Z

2. Sample answers: a) couch, grouch b) clown, down, frown c) sour, hour d) fowl, cowl, owl e) round, ground f) shower, flower g) mouth h) proud i) mouse

Spelling Week 18 – Words with an *s* Sound: c and *s*, pp. 70–71

1. a) passage b) switch c) thirsty d) minus e) whistle f) obtuse g) tinsel h) prince i) space j) request

Answers

Spelling Week 18 – Word Study, p. 72
1. a) organism, reason b) browser, pause c) clothes, cookies d) claws, present
2. a) winged nocturnal animal that eats insects b) wooden or metal object used to hit a ball c) soft, heavy grey metal d) show the way or guide someone to a place e) tall bird with long legs and a long neck f) tall machine used to pick up and move large or heavy objects on a construction site g) drop fo salty liquid from a human's eye h) rip apart **Note:** The order of the answers for a and b, and for e and f don't matter because the pairs of words are identical. It is only important that children choose the correct definitions.

Spelling Week 18 – Word Study, p. 73
1.

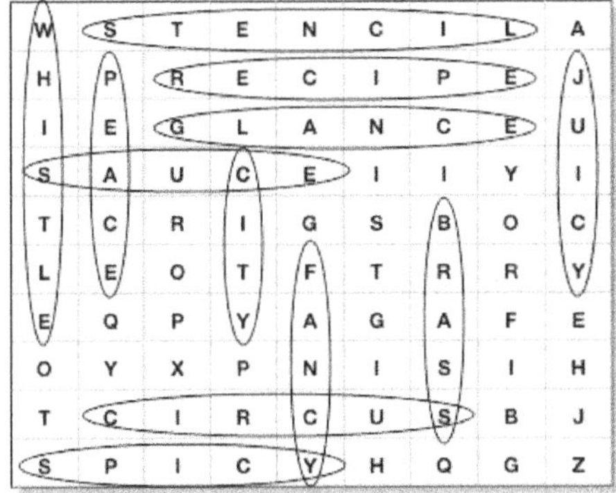

2. Sample answers: a) lift, gift, rift b) mice, nice, spice c) glance, lance, prance, ants, dance
d) mist, missed, fist e) lace, face, race, case, space, trace, grace f) mess, bless, caress g) pest, messed, best, rest, nest h) loose, moose, goose, caboose i) spider, rider, strider, wider, divider

Spelling Week 19 – Words with a *j* Sound: g and j, pp. 74–75
1. a) reject b) fragile c) bridge d) digital e) gerbil f) Ecology g) juggle h) energy i) jewel j) engineer

Spelling Week 19 – Word Study, p. 76
1. a) angry, girl b) organize, giggle c) gear, gift d) geese, piggy, finger
2. a) the study of crime and criminals b) the study of the Earth, its substance, history, and the processes that act on it c) the study of fossil animals and plants d) the study of the atmosphere to forecast the weather e) the study of volcanoes f) the study of birds g) the study of reptiles and amphibians h) the study of skin disorders

Spelling Week 19 – Word Study, p. 77
1. a) jewel b) energy c) juggle d) bridge e) gerbil f) fragile g) engineer h) ecology i) region j) reject
2. Sample answers: a) jacket, jingle, jungle, jump, jive b) fudge, nudge, budge, edge, ledge, age, rage, sage, dodge, danger, range, ranger, stranger c) ginseng, ginger, giant, gigantic, digit, contagious, d) smudgy, fudgy, edgy, spongy, strategy, technology, apology

Spelling Week 20 – Words with an *f* Sound Spelled *ph, gh,* and *f*, pp. 78–79
1. a) enough b) inflate c) rough d) elephant f) amphibian g) surface h) offer i) orphan j) tough

Spelling Week 20 – Word Study, p. 80
1. Sample answers: a) ice cubes; icicles b) firey orange ball; fireball c) perfume; heaven
d) warm hug; cozy blanket e) butterflies; fairies; dancers f) a wild horse; a raging lion g) crashing cymbals; drum rolls
2. a) scratchy b) strong
3. a) cry b) real

Spelling Week 20 – Word Study, p. 81
1.

S	T	U	F	F	I	N	G	A
A	P	H	I	D	M	N	O	V
K	H	C	O	U	G	H	P	K
M	O	F	A	N	G	S	H	Y
U	N	R	H	Y	P	H	E	N
F	E	O	M	W	T	X	R	G
F	L	U	F	F	Y	D	F	E
L	Y	P	H	O	T	O	I	H
E	N	Y	M	P	H	M	S	J
R	O	U	G	H	Y	U	G	Z

2. Sample answers: a) half, staff b) tough, fluff, cuff, stuff, enough c) lace, race, brace, case, mace d) sheet, wheat, meet, concrete, sweet, beat e) judge, grudge f) alone, shown, crone, blown, thrown g) linx, stinks, inks, sinks, rinks, minks h) pinch, winch, cinch i) smile, while, isle, aisle

Spelling Week 21 – Consonant Digraphs: *ch, sh, th,* and *wh*, pp. 82–83
1. a) whine b) channel c) clothes d) archer e) crusher f) nowhere g) gather h) finish i) within
j) kitchen

Spelling Week 21 – Word Study, p. 84
1. a) bench b) thunder c) shingles d) fifth e) dish f) chimp g) which h) cheap i) thing j) whisper
k) splash l) whale or shale
2. Sample answers: a) whip, ship, chip b) chick, thick c) wish, with d) chat, that, what e) then, when f) chin, shin, thin g) cheat, wheat h) chose, those, whose

Spelling Week 21 – Word Study, p. 85
1. a) finish b) crusher c) within d) archer e) clothes f) gather g) whine h) nowhere i) channel
j) kitchen
2. Sample answers: a) chicken, change, chair, chin, charm, chase, chick, bench, watch, itching b) shine, shadow, sharp, shack, shin, shrimp, shift, wish, fish, sunshine c) thing, thin, think, this, that, thumb, thrifty, thirsty, without, fifth, worth d) whistle, who, what, when, where, why, which, whether, nowhere, anywhere

Answers

Spelling Week 22 – Consonant Blends: *scr, spl, spr,* and *str*, pp. 86–87
1. a) scream b) split c) stroller d) sprinkle e) scrape f) scratch g) structure h) splinter i) sprig
j) stranger

Spelling Week 22 – Word Study, p. 88
1. a) tuna, blew, true b) glue, crew, fruit c) pool, loose, due d) review, soup, loom
2. a) stood, could, look b) soot, should, woof c) hood, wood, pull d) cookie, brook, foot
3. a) S b) N c) L d) L e) N f) S g) N h) S i) L

Spelling Week 22 – Word Study, p. 89
1.

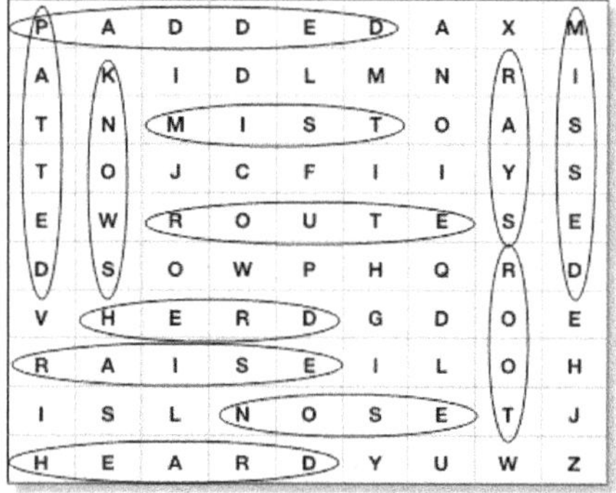

2. a) scrunch b) street c) spritz d) stream e) scrub f) splat g) script h) sprayer i) strength j) sprout k) stripes l) spread

Spelling Week 23 – *R*-controlled Vowels with *or, er, ir, ur,* and *ear*, pp. 90–91
1. a) thirty b) sports c) during d) force e) early f) heard g) nervous h) person i) squirm j) turkey

Spelling Week 23 – Word Study, p. 92
1. Sample answers: a) whirr, fir, stir, sir; sire, fire, wire, tire, expire b) term, germ, fern c) blur, purr, sure, burst, burn, burp, during, fury, curl; bury, four, pour, course, court, source, lure d) worm, world, word, worse, worst, work; born, torn, tore, sore, shore, more, sorry, four, for, fourteen e) learn, heard, pearl, early, earth, earthquake; bear, clear f) were; where, nowhere, here, mere, sphere, adhere, severe
2. a) root b) creek c) do d) mood e) pail f) knot g) hire h) would i) here j) deer k) paws l) plane

Spelling Week 23 – Word Study, p. 93
1. a) person b) during c) force d) early e) squirm f) nervous g) heard h) thirty i) turkey j) sports

Spelling Week 24 – *R*-controlled Vowels with *ar, are, or,* and *ore*, pp. 94–95
1. a) parents b) shore c) care d) farmer e) chores f) parcel g) gorilla h) cart i) factory j) monitor

Spelling Week 24 – Word Study, p. 96
1. a) born b) fork c) hare d) import e) mark f) part
2. You may wish to invite children to share some of their sentences with the class.

Spelling Week 24 – Word Study, p. 97
1.

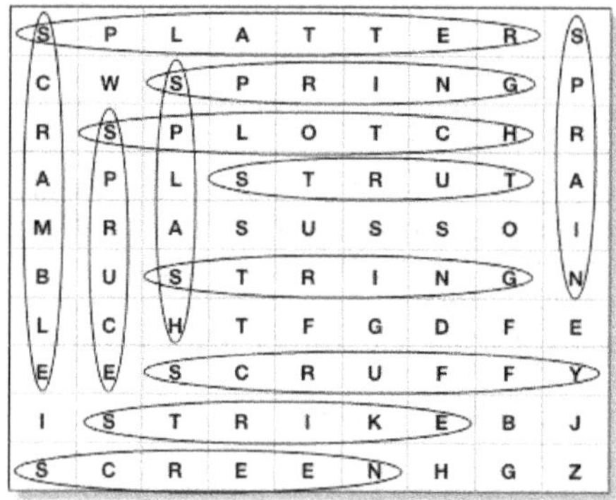

2. Sample answers: a) swore, wore, store, shore, more b) lark, mark, ark c) worn, born, corn, morn d) care, hair, hare, fair, fare, scare, stare, share, spare e) fort, court, port, sort f) carp, harp g) ford, bored, award, lord, scored h) ferret, merit i) fork, pork

Spelling Week 25 – Homographs and Homophones, pp. 98–99
1. a) knight b) peace c) right d) piece e) read f) knew g) new h) night i) reed j) write

Spelling Week 25 – Word Study, p. 100
1. a) aunt b) band c) stair d) fined e) higher f) bored g) maid
2. a) hare b) stare c) pale d) sail e) reel f) reed g) heal

Spelling Week 25 – Word Study, p. 101
1.

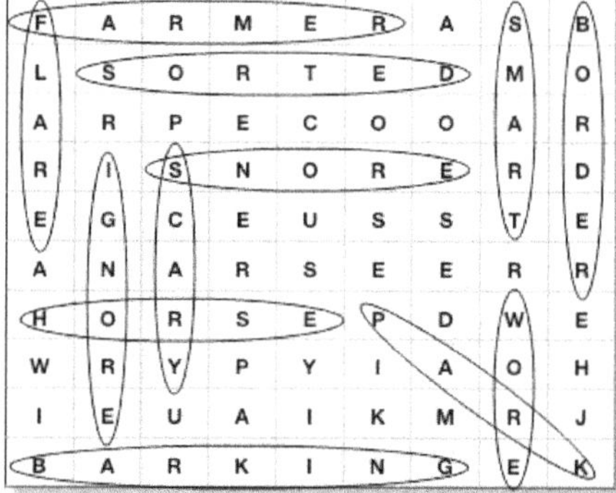

2. a) sharp-tipped object that is shot with an arrow b) bend down gracefully to show respect c) type of bird similar to a pigeon d) dived down

www.ingramcontent.com/pod-product-compliance
Lightning Source LLC
Chambersburg PA
CBHW081342090426
42737CB00017B/3261

9781771055697